LIVING

A

RESTORED LIFE

Proof There Is
An After This

LIVING

A

RESTORED LIFE

Proof There Is
An After This

Kimberly McWilliams

Ordering Information
Please contact Kimberly McWilliams at www.kvmglobal.com or kvmministries2015@gmail.com.

Editor
Lita P. Ward, The Editorial Midwife
LPW Editing & Consulting Services, LLC
www.litapward.com

Publisher
H.O.P.E. Publishing
P.O. Box 28585
Henrico, VA 23228

ISBN: 9780578685571

Table of Contents

Dedication

I wish to dedicate this book to those who love me and to those who hate me. Both have pushed me to be where God already destined me to be. So glad you can't kill whom and what God has anointed to live!

Special Dedication

To my Spiritual Father in Heaven,

Apostle George W. Cooke III

If I had more time to tell you thank you, I would thank you for believing in me, for encouraging me, and for every time you corrected me. There was no way I was going to get away without getting that last one. If I had more time, I would thank you for being a true spiritual father in my life. In it, you taught me the true meaning of being a daughter. If I had just one more second, I would ask you every question I waited until later to ask and get just a little bit more instruction for this journey I must take. I think if I had just a little more time, I would tell you how much I love and appreciate you. Then I would say I hope I've been a fraction to you, of the whole you've been for me. It was recently I stopped thinking if I had more time and realized each day God gives me, is me having that one more time. So, I place a special dedication in here to you. Dad, I hope I am making you proud.

Acknowledgements

First, I give all honor and glory to God above. Without Him, I would be nothing and with Him I shall become. Thank you God for keeping me and for leading me every step of the way. To my three (mom, Adrienne & Lannice), I love each of you very much. Thank you for being my greatest support system. For every night you tolerated me pacing the floor creating, to the times I closed myself in to pour out, I can't appreciate you enough. Thank you babies for allowing mommy the time to leave you a legacy. To everyone else that has a constant hand in my journey, I want to take this time to thank you. As I always say, I dare not call names, for fear of leaving someone out. You know who you are and for all that you do, I am eternally grateful. My life is the better because of you. That's a gift I will cherish forever. Love you!

INTRODUCTION

I believe this is the hardest thing I've ever done in my life thus far. For you, who is reading this and know me, possibly find that quite hard to believe, since time behind bars would out trump that. On the contrary, being open about my life, must be at the top of my list. Even as I'm sitting here, I must be honest, this is Take 5 or 6 of me trying to write this. I would start it and stop. Start again and then stop. All because I couldn't make it through without crying. The blessing for you though, the book you purchased, is not stained with my tears. Plenty of pages were wet from what flowed from my eyes. I must admit, with every typed word, a sense of release came to my life. I've always submitted myself as the sacrifice, the example, that God could use. And just my luck, He took me up on my offer. So, here we are today, with a collection of my thoughts, intertwined within the stories of my life. It is my prayer, that with the turn of each page, something I will say will impart into your life and you, too, will find a sense of release in yours. Enjoy!!

~Kimberly McWilliams~

"Other people are going to find healing in your wounds. Your greatest life messages and your most effective ministry will come out of your deepest hurts."

~Rick Warren

~Once Upon A Time~

Here is the truth to my Fairy Tale...

FAMILY

"Family isn't always blood. It's the people in your life who want you in theirs; the ones who accept you for who you are. The ones who would do anything to see you smile & who Love you no matter what."

This quote about family is so true. Well, at least that's the reality for me. For a long time, it was a sad reality, but now it's a truth that brings me great joy. If it wasn't for those who call me family, I think I would be living a real, lonely existence. I say real because many people feel lonely and really aren't alone. It's a bad feeling to be surrounded by tons of people and still feel like you have no one. As I'm writing now, I can honestly say I've lost count of how many times I've felt lonely, when really not alone. I'm sure you, who are reading this, would say, "But wait, you have people that love you." Well let's keep it 100 right here. I've come to learn I do have people that love me for real. There are more for me than against me. As a matter of fact, that's a good stopping point to release that into your life. There really are more *for* you than against you. Even if your circle is small, the value of those in it are great. No matter the quantity of those around, don't allow that to confuse you with the quality of the relationship you have with them. Some surround you simply because they love the glitz of your life. Lord knows they couldn't handle the story of it, if they even tried.

If they really knew what it took you to get here. If they really knew how many mornings, you struggle just to get out of the bed because you'd rather leave your head under the covers. If they really knew what you had to endure to

4

be where you are. The valleys you had to experience and the mountains you had to climb. If they really knew the sacrifice's you made. And I'm not limiting that to tangible things. I'm talking about the sacrifice of your joy and your peace. For every high place they see, they miss the low places you catapulted from. From your pit place, that's were God raised you to dwell in your promised place. The fight that it took, the one you willingly fought, was all because you knew that a due season was guaranteed, if you didn't give up. That one day, and one very soon, your go through would meet its expiration. I dare you to declare, it's happening now!!!

Family...Family...Family. What a word that is. October of 1981, God saw fit to bring me into my family. It's a pretty large family. If you were to see us today, considering how separate we are, you wouldn't believe just how large we really are. My mom is one of six children. I have tons of aunts and uncles and cousins and this and that. Okay, so you get my drift. Here is an illustration of what I was just speaking of. I was surrounded by so many people and yet I still felt alone. I may have been born into a large family but being accepted by them is a completely different story. My mom told me that I was everybody's baby. From the family to the neighborhood, everyone said I belong to them. Now, when I think back on it, how does a girl go from being everyone's something, to everyone's nothing. By the time I was in high school, the tight knit family I once knew, I knew no more. We did almost everything together. Before one holiday could be over, we were already planning the next. Whose house is going to be the hosting house. Oh, and my absolute favorite was the Friday nights I spent up at my aunt's. Fish Fry and cards! You know what I'm talking about. The adults got together and did what they did. Us kids got together and did what we did. We looked forward to playing with one another. Sometimes continuing games, we left from the last time we were together. Children today really have no clue what fun is all about or what it means to use your imagination. Anyway, we were the McWilliams Family. You would have thought we were celebrities because people just wanted to be in our crew. As I grew, I would say in my head, this is not what you want. For a long time, I was blinded to the troubles of our family. To the secrets that we kept. Oh, trust we did that well. Secrets in our family were bad. To this day, they still are. This may seem silly, but nothing was ever discussed. I can remember when my mom and aunt started experiencing health challenges. The doctor would ask them questions concerning our family's medical history and they couldn't answer with certainty. There were certain things we just didn't talk about. It's that old saying, what happens in the house, stays in the house. I teach my children that now. I laugh though, because, to keep it from one another, what a joke. You know I need to take back something I just said. What happens in the house shouldn't remain in the house, if it's killing you. Secrets eat away at your very existence. It's just like a lie, you need another to cover for the last one. And then another and another and so forth. It becomes a cloud that consumes you to where you can't see nothing else but your secrets and lies. I read a book by Kimberla Lawson Roby about a little girl that was being abused in her home. She kept it a secret. It became so bad that it was taking the very life out of her. She was no longer living as a little girl should and her existence was being destroyed. Funny, I can remember a time in my childhood similar to that. Thinking back, I was so naïve, but I was supposed to be. I was a child and he knew better. In the blink of an eye, I was in the arms of someone I trusted, having my very innocence tampered with. If it wasn't for my grandmother, I have no clue how far it could have gone. I kept it a secret at first, that is, until I couldn't hold it any longer. I told my mommy. She has always been my superhero. Still is today. When I was first locked up, I didn't want anyone to know I was there. You're probably saying because I was embarrassed. To be honest, I hadn't gotten pass the shock of the judge sentencing me, that I didn't embrace any other emotion. I didn't want it told because, in my mind, I wasn't going to be there long. So, it didn't need to be told. It was a secret that got me there and now here I was creating more secrets to cover that one up. That secret didn't just take from me, but it robbed my family too. I'm talking about my mom and my two children. Even my relationship, at the time, suffered because the man I stood beside, couldn't find the courage to stand beside me. Funny how people will turn on you, when the tables are turned on them. He was supposed to be my family and I needed him. I made him my everything and I wasn't even an option to him. To this day, I hate that I put my mom through that. The pain I saw in her eyes, from having no one to walk this with her. So much put on her in a blink of an eye, all because of my secrets. I do believe there are some things that should just go with you to the grave. However, there are things that we keep secret because we don't have the courage to face them. I couldn't face the fact that I was locked up. See that would be me having to conclude I did something wrong and now I'm paying the price. As long as I kept it secret, I could create whatever I desired to cope with the situation. Revealing it means I had to put myself "on front street", as people say. This is normally the place where you lose people because they don't like accountability conversation. I'm going to leave that alone for now. But we will revisit this later in the book.

Where was I? The mask, that most, if not all, of us were wearing, eventually came off when my grandmother passed. Truth be told, the family started falling apart before then. At this point, I was so on the outs with my family, I guess it wasn't supposed to matter. It really did. My first feelings of rejection did not start from outsiders but from those right in my camp. Like I said we were a close-knit family. Once upon a time it seemed we had a bond that no one could break. I believe that's where my foundation of loyalty came from. For a time, we were loyal to one another. Don't you dare talk about or come for any one of us. Coming for one means you just came for us all. Whatever happened to people like that? Times for us were good but when things went bad, they went bad. The love that we showed one another dwindled little by little, until all that seem to dwell was hurt, hate and confusion. It became clear to me, the ones that should be my fans, really were my foes. As badly as I want to believe otherwise, my heart just can't be convinced of it. The concluder of that for me came when my mother and I was put out of my grandmothers (oh that's a story in itself) and no one in the family opened their doors to us. Yeah that pretty much seals it for me. If it wasn't for the kindness of a stranger, my mother and I would've had nowhere to go. Homeless, with a family.... go figure. School and work were on one side of town. Our living quarters was completely on the opposite. I remember the strategy my mom had to come up with just to make sure I made it to school on time and her to work. In the afternoon, I would take a bus to a neighborhood, that would place me close enough to her job, so that I could walk down and meet her. My mommy and I gave the term "black sheep of the family" a whole new meaning. I thank God so much for how he preserved my heart. The way I love people today, instead of hating them, surprises me sometimes. I'm almost positive, as you read this, you can agree with me there. The way God has us built, we still love, when God knows we could hate. I tell people all the time, there are certain things I would love to say no to but the way my obedience to God is set up, I still say yes.

One of my favorite illustrations of family's comes from Genesis 37, with my main man Joseph. The bible says that Joseph was disliked by his family, or should I specifically say his brothers. The bible is quoted in Genesis 37 :4 NKJV to say, "But when his brothers saw that their father loved him more than all his brothers, they hated him and could not speak peaceably to him." Let me first say that

Joseph was born into some very interesting circumstances. It was other children there, that were birthed by other women, and they were all trying to dwell together. Can I attest that I was born into a very interesting circumstance? I was born into a single parent home. There are so many people that make it happen without the assistance of a companion and my mom is one of those ladies. She was that one Tupac talked about who could 'make a dollar out of fifteen cents'. Despite the fact she made it happen, it still wasn't always the easiest of times. I remember this apartment we lived in. It was a nice place, in a quiet to semi-quiet area. Just enough rooms, just enough space but wait, did I mention, just enough roaches too? It wasn't that we were dirty or that we were overrun with bugs, but our neighbors were a different story. They were so nasty that their filth ran out into the hallway, which plagued us who lived within that building. Anyone that knows anything about bugs, knows, that no matter how much you may clean, if those around you are dirty, then you will seem dirty too. Oh gosh, I remember this one time we had a Minister visit from the church and a roach thought it would make its grand appearance. It manages to park itself on the ceiling, right above the minister's head, the whole time he was there. My mom was having a fit on the inside, I just know it. I, being a child on the other hand, thought it was hilarious. Funny thing is, when the minister left, so did Mr. Buggy. So many great adventures in that place. What made me love it the most, it was a place we could call our own. Many of us can attest to not being born into the easiest of circumstances. Someone may say, I was born, too, into a single parent home. Or your story maybe I was raised by my grandparents, aunt/uncle. It could be that you were adopted. It could be that you were raised in the projects or in an abusive home. Spent most of your life in foster care or juvenile detention. A story doesn't have to be the same to still be a story and we all have one. Can I say how glad I am our beginning does not determine our ending. As the bible says in 2 Corinthians 2:14 KJV, "Now thanks be unto God, which always causeth us to triumph in Christ..." My beginning, your beginning, may have not always been happy, but our ending shall be. Haggai 2:9 NKJV says, "The glory of this latter temple shall be greater than the former, says the Lord of hosts. And in this place I will give peace, says the Lord of hosts." I'm so glad that God is the author of my story. Aren't you? That our latter days shall be greater. They shall be filled with joy and with peace. That whatever was hard, God will make easy. That whatever was a struggle, God will smooth and cause the storms to cease. That our worst days are behind and our better days are ahead. No, our best days are NOW! Hallelujah!!

Aside from Joseph being born into an interesting family, he then was overly loved by his father. The bible says that he was his father's favorite. I may have been the only for my mom, but I was beloved by many. I already told you I was the neighborhood baby. Even when my grandmother used to keep me and my cousins, I remember her telling me one day that I was her favorite. I thought that was hurtful because, even at a young age, I understood how that would make the others feel. Truly that was a hear and don't hear moment. Good thing for me, my cousins and I had a solid relationship. Growing up, one of my desires was to buy a home for my cousins and I to live in. Being the oldest out of us four (eventually five), I felt it necessary that I be the protector. My grandmother wasn't always kind to us. Many days I took on things just to keep her from lashing out at them. For a while, my older cousins from New York, would come down and spend summers with us. I remember one summer, something really bad happen between my older cousins and my grandmother. To say what specifically, I can't because I wasn't privy to go behind the closed doors. What I do know is, when my cousins returned to New York, they told my aunt they didn't want to come back and they never did. I told you, I always felt it necessary to protect my younger cousins. Well inside, I looked to my older cousins to protect me. With them leaving, I was left questioning, who was going to protect me now? It wasn't until recently, having a conversation with my mom, I realized that started to shape my distance between them. I needed them and they just left me. I know we were kids but who was going to be there for me. I looked up to them, especially my girl cousin, and now I was alone again. It was later we came to know that my grandmothers Dementia (a form of Alzheimer's) was starting to set in, which is what caused her to act as she did. As a child you don't understand all of that. Just like when my great grandmother took her teeth out and her hair off, on one of our family trips. My cousin ran screaming out of the room because he didn't understand any of that. It was funny to us (still is) but devastating to him. While we couldn't medically deduce her issue, our hearts concluded something wasn't right with how our grandmother treated us. We would try to tell our parents but, true to form, they wouldn't believe us. It's just like one of my favorite childhood songs, by DJ Jazzy Jeff & The Fresh Prince, Parents Just Don't Understand. That was one of my most played cassettes. I played it so much one time, the ribbon started to come out and I needed to get a pencil to wind it back in. Wait, you don't know nothing about that!! I just showed my age, didn't I?

Just like Joseph, I couldn't help being loved. I feel a run right here. Let me clue about a hundred of you in on something right here. You can't help that you are loved by the Father. I don't mean your mommy or daddy this time. I'm talking about our Father who is in Heaven. There are people right now that don't like you and you've yet to figure out why. When they see you, they turn their heads, suck their teeth and immediately get an attitude. All you did was walk in the room and instantly hate rises in them. Please understand that it's not because you're so cute or you dress so well. It's simply because the glory that radiates off you disturbs them. I want to raise two points right here:

1. You can't help that the Father loves you the way he does. Yes, you have messed up, but He loves you. Yes, you turned right when you should have gone left. Guess what? God loves you. I could give you a list that would fill up this book, of all that I have done, and the fact never changes. GOD LOVES ME and HE LOVES YOU. People would hope that you disqualified yourself, yet He keeps qualifying you the more.

The love of our Father is endless. The bible declares in Romans 8:31-32 NKJV, "What then shall we say to these things? If God is for us, who can be against us? He who did not spare His own Son, but delivered Him up for us all, how shall He not with Him also freely give us all things?" Or how about Romans 8:35-39 NKJV, "Who shall separate us from the love of Christ? Shall tribulation, or distress, or persecution, or famine, or nakedness, or peril, or sword? As it is written: *'For Your sake we are killed all day long; We are accounted as sheep for the slaughter.'* Yet in all these things we are more than conquerors through Him who loved us. For I am persuaded that neither death nor life, nor angels nor principalities nor powers, nor things present nor things to come, nor height nor depth, nor any other created thing, shall be able to separate us from the love of God which is in Christ Jesus our Lord."

This is how I see it. Shall problems, your stress, or people gossiping about you, or your financial problems, or who you slept with, argue with or fight with? No! God saw your end in your beginning, and NOTHING shall separate you from His love.

2. You can't help when God decided to raise you and release you. The bible said that Joseph was born in Jacobs old age. And following, its penned, Joseph had a dream. The issue I notice we have with family, and even our friends, is that they "remember when" too much. Sometimes they are so consumed with remembering when that they miss who you are now. See they remember the hoe, but they miss you are now a CEO. People know of my divorce, people know of me having a child out of wedlock (with a man in the church), people know that I did almost two years in jail, people may even know I've filed bankruptcy because I completely tilted the scale of poverty. People know this and people know that, but God still raised me up. It doesn't matter what people think of you, my question is, what does God know concerning you? It wasn't my family that taught me that principle, but my faith in the word of God. You better hold your head up and not hang it down in shame. You have done this, and you have done that, but you are the decider

17

if that will be the end of your story. Will that be all that is ever told about you? For some, what you've done is all they will ever see. However, don't make that your conclusion. In due time, God is promised to raise us all up. Joseph didn't learn this directly from his family but indirectly by their actions. They were the main ones that was trying to push him down. For many of you, the treatment of your family set the stage for how you started out in life. It's what they did or did not teach you that shaped your start.

Can I jump to another story really quickly? How about David and Goliath. First, if you study, you will come to find that David and Goliath were cousins. When Orpah turned back (sister of Ruth, who is mother of David), she eventually had a son. Here we have cousins battling it out. Or how about David and his brother Eliab. David was simply down at the camp, where his father sent him to be, inquiring about beating the giant. Here Eliab gets mad at David. He addresses him based on what he thought about him, not as who God had destined David to be. After all their ranting and raving, in the end,

David shut them all up. The one who thought he was big, bad and better, got his head chopped off. The brother who thought he was so great because he walked with the King, ran in fear, and got to see just who David really was. Sometimes walking with someone, instead of in the anointing God gives you, causes you to lose sight of who you are. In turn, you will also miss the tailor-made blessings God has for you. Didn't you know, some are disturbed right now because yours didn't happen like theirs? They expected your process to match theirs; for you to come into your blessings just like they received theirs. How wrong are they? Let them run their mouths and think what they wish. Just like the outcome of this story, they will come to see just who God has made you to be. That it's not about their timing but God's. Saul tried that on David but David refused. Some are disturbed right now because yours didn't happen like there's. Let them run their mouths. Let them think what they wish. Just like the outcome of this story, they will come to see just who God has made you to be.

Let me pop back to Joseph. The moral at the end of his story is so simple and sure; no matter the pit, the Potiphar or the prison, God will surely raise you up. Can I bless you right here? Even when Joseph was placed in the prison, the palace was above him. Potiphar thought his actions was hindering Joseph. When in actuality, it just placed him right where God destined him. Lord I feel like running again. What people fail to realize, and I say people because I don't want to limit this to any one somebody, but what they fail to realize is their choices forced you into the posture for God to choose you. Their actions pushed you right where God desired to plant you. The moment we made God our choice, is the moment He was able to show us we were always His choice. May I please place Psalm 121 NKJV right here:

"I will lift up my eyes to the hills- From whence comes my help? My help comes from the Lord, Who made heaven and earth. He will not allow your foot to be moved; He who keeps you will not slumber. Behold, He who keeps Israel shall neither slumber nor sleep. The Lord is your keeper; The Lord is your shade at your right hand. The sun shall not strike you by day, Nor the moon by night. The Lord shall preserve you from all evil; He shall preserve your soul. The Lord shall preserve your going out and your coming in. From this time forth, and even forevermore."

Right now, you don't even know the blessing in the midst of your lesson. You might be holding on to hurts they cause. You might still remember every detail of everything they did to you. Lord knows I have some stories, but maturity said, thank them. Thank you for causing me to look up. I came to trust in God. I came to love instead of hate. Thank you for causing me to bless those who curse me. You may have dropped me, but God raised me. I dare you to shout right where you are GOD RAISED ME!! You say to me, "Woman of God, I'm not there yet." Then I dare you to prophesy into your future, GOD SHALL RAISE ME!!

After my grandmother died, everything with our family changed. Even present day, I can honestly say, there are some relatives I haven't seen in 10+ years. Some have even died before I saw them again. It wasn't until recently that I realized, there is a piece of me that is missing, and it lies in them. Don't get me wrong, there are some relatives I can truly do without. I giggled typing that but if you are honest with yourself, we all have that one family member that we duck. I have an uncle that constantly keeps confusion stirred up within the family. He never seems to be caught up in anything positive but whenever something goes wrong, his name is certain to be in the equation. I think he is the main reason we are so divided today. No, I know he is the reason we are so divided today. I reflect on the day of my grandmother's funeral. We were so divided, and the tension was so high, I'm surprised a fight didn't break out. Even present day, we are going through something in our family, and he is the main one causing confusion again. I said to God recently, we are a family that is filled with so much power. If we were to really come together in prayer, trusting and believing you, I am certain that a miracle would show up. So sad, if it was left up to us, we would never see one. I'm so glad that's not how the wonder working power of God operates. Can I tell you, we got our MIRACLE!! See, what God has for you is for you, no matter who seems to be against it. You can't kill what God has anointed to live. It doesn't take many for a miracle. Just two who will touch and agree on any one good thing. You've been looking for a multitude to do this and God said it doesn't take many for your miracle. Just those who truly believe.

For years, this rift in my family did not matter to me, or so I thought, until Father's Day 2018. That day a place in me finally felt empty. I had shared with you that I grew up in a single parent home. At the age of 12 that changed for me. My stepdad, or who I know and call my dad, came into my life. He brought the security and strength that all girls really desire to have, if they are honest with themselves. My dad is the best! He has been there through everything in my life. While I can't think of a moment my dad wasn't there and how great he is, I didn't realize just how much he meant to me fully until that year. 2018 was the year I thought of every Father/Daughter dance I missed. How many plays I didn't have a dad in the audience. Oh, please don't miss a very important fact I stated before, my mom is my A1. She is so many things to me, I don't think I could even express them all. Inside there was a hole, an empty space, that I didn't even know was there. Oh, my love, there are some places inside of you, right now, that are empty. You don't even know it anymore because you've numbed yourself to it. Maybe you've tried to fill it with everything else, so that you don't have to feel the ache of it. I know it all too well. Father's Day 2018, I was posting about my great dad and tears came to my eyes. While reflecting over the missing things, I started to replay all the things my dad was there for. The day he walked me down the aisle, he held my arm so tight, I wondered did he change his mind in giving me away. The day of my graduation, I looked out in the audience and he was sitting right there. Every degree on my wall has my dad's support, push, hugs, you can do this, attached. I'm tearing up now as I write this. My absolute favorite memory is when I was in a play in school. I played Frenchy from Grease. That character was a beauty school girl. So, you know what that means? Wigs Wigs and more Wigs. I can see it right now just as if it was yesterday. The nights he would let me place my wigs on his head and style them for my play. The nights he would let me polish his toe nails so that I could perfect my skills for cosmetology class. I almost want to stop writing, right now, so I can call him and tell him thank you. I know my Dad story may not be your story. I want to help you with your empty place right here. Now this is only for the select few. While he is my dad in every sense of the word, at the same time he wasn't (biologically). I remember the night that I heard him and my mom arguing behind closed doors. I was still a teenager, but I made it a point to join a grownup moment. I heard my mom say stop one too many times and before I knew it, I burst into the room and took a swing at him.

In a reflex motion, he hit me back. I can still hear the ringing in my ears that lasted for quite some time. Sure, I'm standing up for my mom but that was also me not staying in a child's place. To this day, I can't remember how our relationship was right after that because we have always been so close. Here is why we are so close. My dad loves me despite my mom. He loves me, after their divorce. To not have him at home every day did hurt, but his constant presence made it all better. He never changed. He's still there for everything. I can come home now and find him in my yard, cutting my grass. It was that very thing that made me appreciate him so much. I know I'm speaking of my dad, but the main point here is genuine love. Just as the quote said in the beginning, family is not determined by who you are born in to but those who really are there for you. Those that know you and still love you. That have seen your flaws and still love you. That heard the rumors about you and still love you. I remember the night I turned myself in to the authorities. The look on my parent's face is one I will never forget. I can see the one on my dad's face, and it breaks my heart right now. It was almost like he didn't recognize the woman he was looking at; not his princess. Not his little girl. Not the one he raised. Not the church girl. Just as confused as he looked, in a blink of an eye, a calm came over him and he went to planning how to get me through one more thing. Genuine love has no limit, nor does it have stipulations. If you think about it, you have someone in your life now or before, that you know gave you genuine love. My dad came into my life to restore something my family took from me, that I didn't even know was so important to me. He came to show that there is purpose inside of me. He came to show me that I do matter and that I am deserving of love. I remember when he first stepped on the scene, I was unsure about him. Hey, it was just me and my mom for 13 years of my life and now there was one more. The way he came into my life should have told me how he would be for the rest of my life. It was when we were at a hard place. He pretty much rescued us and that's who he has been my whole life.

Think about where you were at a certain point of your life. What you were dealing with or who you were surrounded by? Maybe you reflect on who wasn't there or what you didn't have? You have it in mind? Now if you really think about it, who was it that came into your life or stepped up at that point in your life, that gave you the genuine love you deserved? See you were so consumed by what you didn't have that you missed what you did. That's what hit me two years ago. Not the dances he missed but the ones he made. Not the days I don't see him, but the days I do.

Above all, he never made me feel less a part of him, even though I didn't carry his name. Today reflect on those who you call yours and they proudly call you theirs. They find no shame in being connected to you. That's real love.

The family I was born in to taught me a lot about life. It's my born-again family, though, that has taught me to live. There are so many things of my story I would love to tell about them. My stance to this day, is that my grandmother's death was a murder. It doesn't matter that the killers are family. What they did pushed her to her death and again, it became another secret we have. I'll leave that where it is but that's a secret, fifteen years later, that still hurts. I truly believe their rejection caused me to gravitate to the church for fulfillment, and sadly I didn't find it there. What I needed to find first had to start within me. We dance and shout over the recovery of Job, double for our trouble, but there is a key revelation many miss in the story. The understanding of the word "recovery" in Job 42, is to turn away from captivity. Here's my point. While God may have given him back the material things, Job was no longer bound to them. His recovery relinquished his captivity to them. Take my car, my house, my money, touch what you may devil, but you can't touch my peace or my certainty in God. Job lost everything and while he could have, even was encouraged to deny God, he never did. You must become so rooted and grounded in your relationship with God that no matter what the devil touch, he can't take your joy, your peace, or your certainty in God. Can I paint an even greater picture of his commitment to God? The bible says that God told his negative friends to go to Job for prayer. Wait! Not the ones that tried to talk him out of his blessing. The ones that talked crazy to him, instead of comforting him. The ones who could have made things worse for him. Those are the ones you want him to pray for? In our world, not the family that talked about me and my mom. Not the ones that left us out there for dead and could care less what happen to us. Those are the ones God? How about your testimony? No, not the father or mother I never came to know because they weren't present in my life. Not the one that abused me. Not the one that took from me. Not those that dropped me or stabbed me in the back. And the list goes on.

"Yes," God said. "That's the one that I'm calling you to pray for."

And Job prayed. His obedience to God meant more than the discouragement of man. It took me a long time to get there but I now reside in that place. Job lived a great life and in an instant, he lost it all. In the end, God gave him back all and then some. It wasn't until he prayed for his friends, that God restored him. It wasn't until he did the hard thing that God made his load easy. I don't know where you stand with your family. Maybe it's not your family, as in aunt/uncle, sister/brother, but maybe it's in a husband or a wife. It may be a childhood friend or best friend. As we are concluding this chapter, whomever you have strain with or even had an aught with that you never let go, before you turn the page, I want you to conclude it now. God can't restore you until you let go. Out of you doing the hardest thing, God said I can make your load easy. Matthew 11:29-30 KJV, "Take my yoke upon you, and learn of me; for I am meek and lowly in heart: and ye shall find rest unto your souls. For my yoke is easy, and my burden is light." He can't lift it, if you don't let Him have it. When God restores, He is taking you out of captivity. It will no longer trouble your dreams. It will no longer disrupt your peace. It will no longer weigh on your heart. It took me 10 years to see some of my family again. I remember the last day I saw them and how I knew I would possibly never see them again. Forever to see them wasn't long enough because of the anger I felt towards them. Somewhere along the way my anger turned into missing. I started to remember how close we were and how much fun we use to have; the trips we took together and the summers we spent. There was a piece of me in them. Finally, I did it. I let go and I reached out. Sure, today we are not where we use to be, but my heart is freer than it's ever been. I have a peace now that no one can disrupt. Forgiveness doesn't mean we will come together again. Forgiveness simply says I release you so that I can be free. Before you turn the page, do just that. Free yourself. Then when you turn the page, make that a signifying movement that I'm turning the page on that. God is turning your captivity from the very thing that held you bound; the very thing that shackled your moves; the very thing that plagued your mind and kept captive every thought. God says He is freeing you right now. He is turning your table. He is writing an alternative ending to that part of your story. He's just been waiting on you. Family, it's time to be free.

JOURNAL YOUR THOUGHTS

Coming out of the chapter of me sharing my intimate thoughts and moments concerning family, how do you feel or what are your thoughts? What are some personal confessions you will make before you turn the page?

_____

_____

_____

_____

_____

_____

_____

_____

_____

_____

_____

_____

LOVE

"The heart that's meant to love you will fight for you when you want to give up, pick you up when you're feeling down, and will give their smile when it's hard for you to find yours. They will NEVER get strength from seeing you weak, power from seeing you hurt, or joy from seeing you cry. The heart that's meant to love you wants to see the best of you, not the hurt you! Never forget that.

-Trent Shelton

*L*ove...who would have ever thought that four little words could mean so much? When one thinks about it, what is love? Is it defined to be feelings between a parent and their child? Is it the intimacy that is shared between a man and a woman? Or those who have been the best of friends since childhood? For me, I would have to say, it's been a combination of them all and more. The irony of it all is, love is something that means so much, and yet it has caused me so much pain. Oh, I'm sure I'm not the only one with that story. I already shared with you some of my feelings concerning my family. If it wasn't for my mom, my children and those God blessed my life with, I don't think I would know what the bond of a family really feels like. Through the years, I have had the love of those I called friend. One of my friends now is my best friend and sister all wrapped into one. She, herself, has been through so much and I feel God brought us into each other's lives for an assigned purpose. Isn't that like God? To bring us people that provide exactly what we need, right when we need it. Some come only for a season. Others He will send, are meant to last for a lifetime. The sad part is, when people do come, we get so overwhelmed with their presence, we miss what position they are supposed to play. We hold on to people we should let go and we let go of people, and I mean way too soon, that we should keep. How do we get so tied up like that? It's like the analogy I often use. I believe I did in my last book. When I'm in the grocery store, one of the things that fascinate me, is how many people buy cottage cheese. Honestly, I have never really eaten cottage cheese outside of it in my lasagna. Truthfully, I'm not interested in eating it either. But people eat it like it's the best thing. They add fixings to it and its just yummy yum for them. And every time I notice someone eating it, I think to myself, no matter what they put in it or what you label it, the fact remains it's spoiled milk. We put labels on people and expectations but at the end of the day, just like the cottage cheese, the person or the relationship is nothing more than spoiled milk. It simply is what it is. As believers, we hold out hope for situations until that hope fails us. We see the signs to stop, turn back, go the other way, and we never do any of the above. For this reason, I'm so glad God is who He is. Because when I couldn't seem to get myself out of places, especially those I put myself in, He provided a way of escape. Where people fell off and I never could understand why, I thank Him for severing me from what I couldn't see. When the relationships I kept getting into, repeatedly, that beat me left and right with hurts and disappointment, God kept my heart and my mind. We really serve a great, great God.

For some time now, I have wondered why this topic, of love, is such a struggle for me. I am such a loving person (in my opinion of course) and have a heart that's ready to be loved. Yet, after attempts, I'm just not successful. Being one who internalizes, I had to hold the mirror to my face and ask, God show me me. Many times we say we're ready but are we really? Friends weren't a problem for me because I was a social butterfly. The thing is, the older I got, the less I fit in. As a single parent, my mom did her very best, but I didn't always have on the latest name brand, live in the popular neighborhood or drive the flyest car. As a matter of fact, I wore labels but not those of an average teenager. By high school, my closet housed a wardrobe of about 95% dry clean only clothes, due to adult hand me downs. Certainly, a far stretch from jeans and tees. My first car was a grey Chevrolet Nova. It was a stick shift and honey, you couldn't tell me nothing. I was proud and excited about what my dad gave me. Yet, it was never enough for everyone else. What I wore on my body, or the place I called home, not even the car I drove, discounted the love I housed to give in my heart. At that age, it just didn't work that way. I think sometimes, today, I can hear the taunts of the kids. Especially when I walk the halls of my daughters' high school, being it was the same I went to and graduated from. I question myself on occasion, do I do for my kids, in the manner I do, because I don't want them to endure what I did as a child? Lord knows it's not because I can always afford it. Being a single parent really is a challenge. I just don't want my son teased or my daughter to hide ugly words spoken to her, the way I did. I hid the ugly words because I didn't want my mom's feelings hurt or her to feel she needed to address what I endured at the school. In the church, I had friends, but that even had its challenges. I'll never forget the Sunday, one of the youth, looked me in my face and told me she hated me and didn't know why. CRUSHED is putting it mildly. How can you tell someone you don't like them, no hate them, and don't know why? In my eyes, she had everything. Beautiful clothes, an influential mother, beautiful voice, the love of our Pastor as a father. She seems to do what she wanted, as she wanted, so what was her issue with me. One of the funniest things is how people that seem to have it all, dislike those that don't. I mean they look at us, not even knowing what it took to get here. Trying to make it with the little we have, and they have so much to say. I think about the widow at Zarephath. When the Prophet Elijah came upon her at the gate gathering sticks, she was in a mental state that life was over for her. Just as she was about to throw in the towel, God sends the man of God to come and speak a blessing into her life. He threw that towel right back at her. I'm sure you can testify of the times you wanted to throw in the towel. You tried to throw in the towel but God wasn't having it. You were going to see this to the end.

As I digress, here is why I brought this illustration up. When the Prophet heard what she was to do, he said to her to do as she will but bring him back a drink and some bread first. The woman replied all she had was a little bit of flour and a little bit of oil. Sure, she didn't have what he specifically asked for, but the ingredients she possessed would have made the same. Catch my drift? We discount what we do have because we feel it doesn't meet up or match certain standards. We find ourselves seeking externally for something we already possess inside. So what you don't sing like someone else? God said use your voice. So what you don't preach like the next one? God said release what I have placed in you. So what your business isn't coming together like another? God said go forth in what I've placed in your hand. You will succeed. I didn't need to be like everyone else. God said I want you to be like no one else but who I created you to be. Jeremiah 1:4-10 NKJV says it like this,

> "Then the word of the Lord came to me, saying: 'Before I formed you in the womb, I

knew you; Before you were born, I sanctified you; I ordained you a prophet to the nations.' Then said I: 'Ah, Lord God! Behold, I cannot speak, for I am a youth.' But the Lord said to me: 'Do not say, I am a youth, For you shall go to all to whom I send you, And whatever I command you, you shall speak. Do not be afraid of their faces, For I am with you to deliver you,' says the Lord. Then the Lord put forth His hand and touched my mouth, and the Lord said to me: 'Behold, I have put My words in your mouth, See, I have this day set you over the nations and over the kingdoms, To root out and to pull down, To destroy and to throw down, To build and to plant."

From the very beginning, we are destined to be set a part. That means our square will not fit in every circle. Even when we want to, it's just not a part of our plan. Being set a part keeps us chosen vessels. See anyone can be called, even if by accident. And when called, you can find yourself answering to anything. But when you are chosen, that means you were specifically picked. That, out of options, you were the priority choice. That's what set apart means. I've been specifically chosen, and I carry something different from anyone else. That means I function as the toe and not the hand because that is not my design. I function as the knee and not the teeth because that is not my design. If you're like me, it took me a long time to identify with my design because I was trying to find myself in others. I was always on the outside, trying to find out what would get me on the inside. Even now as an adult, I deal with the same challenges, and for a time I was trying to figure out again how to get inside. Then one day Jeremiah 1 played in my mind again, to where it hit me in my spirit. I didn't anoint you to be others. I anointed you to be you. If you remember nothing else, I say in these pages, please remember, God anointed you to be you. From the crown of your head to the soles of your feet, God fashioned you to be you. Your alignment is to His will and to His way. Your answer is yes Lord I will obey. Your posture is come what may, my answer is yes. You are fearfully and wonderfully made. You are God's most special handiwork. While you may want to fit in, you are designed to set the mark, set the standard, and to stand out.

As a young person, I must admit boys really weren't on my agenda. I believe out of my entire childhood, there was only one boy I had the eyes for. It's funny how my affections became fixated on one person. I've always been one that put all her eggs in one basket. I can sing his name right now, but I leave out names to protect the innocent, as well as the guilty. Can I tell you, even as a teenager, he was so good looking? The boy had arms on him and at the time, I was a thick girl. Not a big woman, like I am today. He could scoop me up in his arms and I would think I'm in La La Land. He was so funny, had a great personality, and he was friends with my friends. The perfect package but there was a teeny tiny problem...he had a girlfriend. Yeah, my Mr. Wonderful was already taken. In high school, I wouldn't say that I was unpopular, but I wasn't on the A-List either. My mom's bank account and our beautiful townhome didn't qualify us, if you catch my drift. To be in the A-List team, you had to have money and be from the right neighborhood. The funny thing is, some of those on that list I knew, but they never fully welcomed me to join. I'll never forget this other young man, who didn't live too far from me. He paid me a lot of attention, but I knew then it was only for one thing. SEX! I enjoyed his attention so much, I use to pretend to be that girl. Get what I mean? The truth was, I knew nothing. So, on one hand I had a guy who seemed to genuinely like me but could only show it privately. Like Xscape said, "I was his little secret." Then I had another, who I knew deep inside thought nothing of me, but I still allowed to con me.

Teenage life...go figure. Either way, bottom line, I experienced REJECTION...AGAIN. From the very beginning, love was always something I had to play a role for. It never seemed that I could be loved for just being myself. It always came with compromising my standards. I grew up in the church and one that had no problems telling you the right things to do. They didn't mind tackling the tough topics, like no sex before marriage. So spiritually, I knew the standard, but I still compromised. I grasped the wrong concept on how to have love in your life. The concept was, anything was better than nothing at all. Doesn't that sound crazy? Lord, I was so wrong. How many of you know true love doesn't settle? It can't because settling makes sense, where love, makes no sense at all.

Let me explain what I mean. We all set standards...the looks, height, teeth, dress, smell...those things that you can check, check, check off your list. These are the sensible things but nothing to make you fly over the moon. Love, on the other hand, may be able to meet your check list, but it also says, if they don't, it's alright. Why? Because, it's something about them that just makes the world spin to the point you can't catch your breath. It's almost terrifying at times because you don't know how you got there, but never want to leave, all at the same time. I'm talking about the love you can't be without and the one you always imagined being with. Love, it is specific. There is no question who. You specifically love this one. You specifically know they are meant for you, even without all the puzzle pieces falling in place. You specifically know they are who you want to do life with. That's real love. No settling, it's sure.

Let's speed up this story. I had finished my freshman year in college, and I was so excited about coming home. Let me tell you freshman year was a year filled with trying to fit in again. I had the chance to go to college early and that summer set the stage for my year to come. I tried to be the party girl and honey, I was good at that. I knew where to club on a Monday and a Wednesday. When you know that, you are one that makes a career out of partying. I dabbled in smoking marijuana and I loved getting my drank on. Lol! Lord, it's been a while since I've said that phrase. I would wake up with something and I would go to bed with something. I was doing my best to blend in and escape simultaneously. Somewhere along the way, I gave up on my academic success. My grades suffered greatly (college was harder than expected) and my self-esteem dropped even lower than it had ever been. I remember experiencing my first, real moments of depression and entertaining thoughts of suicide. When my freshman year ended, the decision was made for me to come home. I made it because my dad said I was missed but deep inside, I did it because I couldn't live life like that anymore. As I sit here now, four degrees later, I can honestly say that decision saved my life.

In my coming home, that's how I met my ex-husband. One of my friends, at the time, was dating this guy in the Navy. It was one weekend, she was invited down to the base, and he asked her to bring a friend. Well, here was the friend (talking about me) front and center. We went down and spent the entire weekend with them, and I had a blast. That friend of his though, I HATED HIM! I thought he was a jerk and I wanted far away from him. Lord, I should have kept with that mindset. After getting home, a few days later my friend shared during her pillow talk, her friend revealed that his friend liked me. I couldn't believe it. There was no possible way because we didn't click at all. I guess the words "opposites attract" were the sentiments of our case. I pondered for a few days after being told how he felt, and I made the decision to reach out to him. My heart, I believe, was so excited that someone expressed interest in me, without the pressure of having sex. Finally, this was happening for me. Things started off good. He was a charmer; sent me roses, which is my favorite flower, and took me out to nice places. We laughed, talked, and just enjoyed one another. I couldn't believe the guy I thought was a jerk ended up being so amazing. Song of Songs 4:7,9 NLT, "You are altogether beautiful, my darling, beautiful in every way. You have captured my heart, my treasure, my bride. You hold it hostage with one glance of your eyes, with a single jewel of your necklace." He made me feel loved and beautiful. The sad part here is I placed my assurance on those feelings solely in him and not already trying to find them within myself. Inside, I was so insecure. Not because of anything he did, but because of the history of rejection I experienced. There were days I convinced myself that he would find someone better than me or that he was cheating on me with someone where he lived, due to the distance. Let me tell you, long distance relationships are hard, and will not work, if you have no trust. I struggled but there was a revelation I gathered today. The one who is truly destined for you is not assigned to complete you but to confirm you. What I mean is, if you didn't love yourself for yourself, how can you comprehend those feelings given by someone else? The moment they stop loving you, there goes your love for yourself. When they come into your life, they come to confirm that you are beautiful, that you are wise, that you are loving, that you are desirable, that you are attractive, that you are kind, that you are a giver, that you are strong. Sure, while with them, there will be things that will come to light. It shouldn't be because they planted it there, but they help bring out what God already placed there. Sometimes when we don't have those around us that can truly see into us, we may miss some of what God has placed inside of us. That is until we encounter the one that brings it out of us. Proverbs 27:17 NLT, "As iron sharpens iron, so a friend sharpens a friend." One of the most famous quotes, handed down to generations, is quoted by Polonius in Shakespeare's Hamlet, "To thine own self be true." Socrates said it a little like this, "To know thyself is the beginning of wisdom." So, what is this wisdom, this truth, that we need to come to embrace?

1. **Happiness/Living A Life of Truth**: there is a joy that comes with acceptance. I was always taught to accentuate the positive, eliminate the negative. When you are always focusing on the negative, you leave yourself in a state of depression. That is a permanent sadness that you walk around with, concerning who you are and your abilities. Coming to appreciate, even the smallest thing, will open the door for you to see greater. In turn, happiness from within will bring happiness from without. I love the way my eyes are shaped. I have such a cute laugh.

Whatever it may be, start with that and work your way to more. Knowing this within yourself will keep you from waiting to hear it from others. I love me today, gives you that assurance until you come to hearing it daily from someone else. Then if that day comes and you don't hear it as often as you desire, you are still not in want. Because you have assured yourself of something that you didn't need another to validate. The bible declares in John 3:16 that God love the world that He gave His son. Let me stop right there. He loves us just that much that He gave of His own life so that we may live. That's love like none other, that He would give of His very breath, so that we may breathe. That's a good reason to have joy. To know that my flaws and all, would cause such a price and He said, "I'll pay that." My God, as the tears are flowing now. I think of the lashes He took for me. I think of the spit He took for me. I think of the torment He took for me. I think of the crushing He took for me. That's an unspeakable joy. Do you know how precious you are to God for Him to do that for you and for me? I have battled with depression. So, I get the dark place. The feeling that the world would be better off without you. And that feeling was not so long ago. But every time I think that, I remember that simple phrase, "God so loved the world that He gave." See every time I see the world without me, I remember that He saw it with me, when He gave His life. If His purpose was not for me to be here, then He wouldn't have died so that I may live. We were counted into His plan. We are a part of His purpose.

2. **Better Decision Making/Resistance to Pressure:** I made some of the worst decisions of my life because of my self-esteem. I remember the night I lost my virginity. I had talked myself to such a place that I had no choice but to go all the way. This person didn't even deserve such a precious gift and honestly, he didn't even know I was giving it to him. Over the years, while I never committed to one set one, I had enough someone's in my camp. None of them really wanted to be with me; they just wanted what they could get from me. I knew this but I went with it anyhow. When you come to know you for real, you don't have to make the

same bad decisions I did, to find completion in someone else. I already told you they don't come to complete, but confirm.

3. **Self-Control/Less Inner Conflict:** I pretty much told you this one in the last. Coming to know myself, I came to know what causes me to do good and to do bad. Paul said, "That what I shouldn't do, that's what I do and what I should, I don't." There is no confusion as to why, when you tap into your motivators. Ask yourself, what motivates me? What makes me happy when I'm sad? What makes me angry and what makes it subside? Here's the big one. What causes my flesh to act up? What's that one song, that one smell, that takes me under? Don't act like you have no clue what I'm talking about. When you know better, you will do better. Tapping in to that place isn't meant to take you back, but to keep you moving forward.

He started off being that for me. He made me feel I was worth the work. That I didn't have to give of myself physically before he got to know the emotional and spiritual side of me. We seemed to be so in love. Key word...SEEMED. I do have to applaud him for pushing me further in my Christian walk. He introduced me to his Pastor and before I knew it, I became a member and I was enrolled in Minister's Class. After several meetings and testing, I was licensed as an Evangelist. I do believe my ex-husband knew I had a serious relationship with God, but I don't think he understood just who I was in God. Can I tell you something crazy? The man that took me to church stop going himself. That's right! On Sundays, he would drive me to the church and drop me off. After the "I Do" it seemed our lives became an "I Don't." Truth is, I knew I didn't love him as a wife the day I moved down there. Yet I stayed and made myself try to make it work. Life was so miserable at times. I would spend my days and nights crying; more on the inside, than I did on the outside. He was so checked out of the responsibilities of life. I remember one winter I spent four days in the middle of a snow storm with no lights and no heat in our apartment. He was so irresponsible with money and it would always be the things that impacted me that he wouldn't pay. I didn't have the heart to go home to my parents. That would have made me a failure. Since I had no one else I could call, I stayed put. The snow was so high; it came up to our window. Two fools stuck inside and freezing. He went out, bought heaters and we had blankets, but what was that really doing? I don't even think we really had groceries in the house. It was a total disaster. And you know what I did when this whole situation passed? I stayed with him. Dumb, right? So many other things happened while we were together. From cars being repossessed to empty bank accounts, it seemed nothing was the deal breaker for me. He never hit me with his fists, but he hurt me in so many other ways. I remember when he asked me to marry him. It was thought out and quite lovely. I think I ended up saying yes because I blacked out. By our wedding day, I still wasn't in love with him. Yet, I went on with it anyway. I convinced myself of every reason why, so that everyone would be happy; everyone except me. *Kim, he will be hurt*, I thought. *All of those people out there*, I thought. Your *parents spent so much money*, I thought. *People have traveled so far*, I thought. And on and on, around and around, the thoughts went. Maybe I did it because I felt this was going to be my only chance. I reverted to that little girl that felt anything was better than nothing. When was my mindset going to change? I really did give it a try as a wife. I remember when I found out I was pregnant with my daughter. I had a long talk with myself again. *Kim, this is your chance to be a wife he desires. You already aborted one baby. Don't do that again.*

Let me take this off ramp for a second. I was so hurt after having an abortion. I never realized how hurt I would be until the procedure was over. I went into it with the mindset I can't bring a child into this. I'm not in love with this man. I barely love him. How can I attach myself to him for life with having a child? I saw it as a death sentence for me and the kid. So I was actually excited and sure until the tiny baby laid as a blob in a tube. One of the greatest things we can do as a woman is bring forth life. The feeling you have with carrying a precious life inside. Feeling it grow and move and develop. To hear their heartbeat at that first appointment, to that first cry they make when they take their first breaths in the world. To count those precious fingers and toes. It's one of the most beautiful times of your life. Something not every woman can do but I could, and I allowed misery to take that from me. It's amazing what you will allow someone to take from you. Something so precious and you let them strip you of it. Many of us abort things and I'm not just speaking of children. We abort dreams, hopes, promises and visions, all because of "they" or "misery". We allow the words of someone to override the words of the one that gave us the gift. God makes no mistakes. We might, but He doesn't. So, if He chose us for the gift, He meant it. He knew who you were when He chose you. He knows who you are when

He chooses you. And He knows who you'll be when He chooses you. After everything, guess what?! HE STILL CHOSE YOU! No one has the right to take something from you that they didn't give you. Never forget that.

Well, back to my baby girl. It was hurricane weather outside and it felt like I was going through a hurricane inside. My emotions were all over the place. I took a trip home to see my parents and deliver the news. As always, they were supportive of whatever my decision was going to be. So, I went forth with the pregnancy, but my marriage didn't come with it. By the time my daughter arrived, we could have been labeled roommates. He started acting more foolish and with each passing day, I felt less and less like his wife. By the time my daughter was six weeks old, our marriage took a nose dive. It was time for me to return to work. I had gotten my daughter dressed and was on my way out the door. I picked her up and she just didn't look right. She began to gag and I remember seeing her eyes somewhat roll to the back of her head. I grabbed the phone and called my husband because I was so scared. He was definitely no help, but he did say something smart. "Call 911" and I did. They came and they helped my baby. We went to the hospital and he met me there. For days, I didn't sleep because I was so scared my baby would stop breathing. Not one of those nights did he sit up with me. Once again, I was alone. He never offered advice or comfort on what to do to get through this. Oh, but he did find time to tell me I wasn't fulfilling my wifely duties. That my place was to be over there in the bed with him and not over in the room with our daughter. That night, tears flowed from my tired eyes, as I rocked our baby. To his correction, I hadn't performed my wifely duties for quite some time. The nights we were having so-called sex, was more me laying there and him on me satisfying himself. I can't remember the last time we just talked about how our days were. The last time we went out together or hung out with our friends. My duties stopped some time ago. All of this and I had no one to share it with. His family didn't like me because let's just say, they came from a different place. They felt as if we were sticking our noses up at them. To this day, that cracks me up. Me, who once upon a time was homeless, thinks less of someone else? Chile please. People really have some colorful imaginations at times. I had no friends down there. My husband wanted me to fit in with the military wives' crew but that just wasn't my thing. Let me tell you about this cookout, we were invited to, that I came to this conclusion. The wives assembled in the living room and the men in the backyard. A stripper showed up for our entertainment! Ummm, okay not such a big deal. That is until one of the ladies pulled the stripper's private part out of his pants. It looked as if she was looking for more than a strip tease. We all got up and left them out in the living room. No, the military wives club was not for me. Certainly, I wasn't going to reach out and tell them anything. They seemed to have their own issues. Why not my family you ask? I couldn't face looking weak to them. I already dealt with rejection from my family since childhood. This would just be one more thing to add to their list and I wasn't going to subject my mom to that. So, I stayed, and my daughter grew. She was a happy baby but not to the extent that I believed she should. Many told me how you are during your pregnancy will affect how your baby will be. Well, here it was in living color for me. I cried a lot during my pregnancy and for some reason, my baby just seemed so sad. Not that she cried, but she didn't smile enough for me. She didn't really talk but there wasn't much of that going on in the house anyway. She could feel something was wrong. It was then I got the courage to talk to my ex-husband. That night, our conversation seemed to go okay, but in a blink of an eye, it went so wrong. It's mind blowing how quickly a conversation can turn physical. I don't remember all of what he did to provoke me, but I remember my response. Somehow, we ended up by the front door and I had uppercut him under his chin.

I don't remember all we were saying but I wanted him to shut his mouth. I didn't want to hear his voice again and those condescending remarks. I didn't want to hear anything stupid or self-centered. I wasn't taking not one more lash from his tongue. I didn't even give a thought to him hitting me back. I just wanted peace. The moment I struck him, I shocked myself and I backed away. In that split second, my marriage was over. We didn't need a judge or divorce decree to tell us that. That moment made it over. He agreed divorce was the best, but by the next morning, he wanted us to work it out. I wanted to say, "Are you a fool? I just struck you and you want to work it out? No sir! No way!"

There weren't enough "I love you's" in the world to make me stay. I packed everything I could fit in my car, including my baby, and I got out of there. I left everything I thought mattered behind, and with every mile I said, "God will give you better, Kim." I thought of every night I wet my pillow with my tears, and I said, "God will give me my joy back." I thought of the bank accounts I lost because he depleted them with his foolish spending habits, and I said, "One day God will give that back to you." I thought of the nights I slept alone, after our daughter got sick, because he cared about his job and I said, "I shall sleep in peace again." I didn't have to lay and perform no more wifely duties. I felt nasty and obligated. Wiping tears from my eyes, I said to myself, "You'll never have to open your legs and do that again." Every time a thought of our lives, came to mind, I just said, "No more."

Can I pause right here for you to say, "No more?" Every thought that comes across your mind, that cripples you, declare, "No more!" Every past memory that haunts your present, declare, "No more!" I know it may feel like a challenge but there's no reason to read my freedom and not receive your own. Paul said, "Forgetting the former things, nevertheless I press." A press is an intentional step. It's not one that's easily made. It might feel as if you are weighted down but nevertheless, I'm still going to make it. You must get to such a place, where you tell your weights, "I'm going to press with you until I press may way out of you. It's heavy right now, but every day I declare my load is getting easier. I won't stay stuck backwards that I miss moving forward. My history will not keep me from reaching my destiny."

On the next page, I'm inserting a space, for you to write what those crippling, hindering thoughts are and then I want you to daily declare over them, "NO MORE!"

YOUR THOUGHTS...

I left and I never looked back. As freeing as it was, it also opened a door to many years of struggle. Can I tell you that with each year of struggle, I never once considered going back to him? Even when he convinced all our so-called friends that I was in the wrong, the thought of going back never crossed my mind. I even heard he was going to get his closest friend to say I was on drugs and that I was an unfit mother. He had the Pastor of our church call me and boy did I get an ear full. Of course, his family couldn't miss their moment chiming in during this time. With all of that, I still never considered reconciliation. I knew, and he knew, we weren't right for each other. The only misfortune in this story is, when our relationship ended, so did the one he decided to have with his daughter. It was 10 years, after we separated, before he really spent time with her. When we first separated, like clockwork, he would have some balloons or flowers delivered for her birthday but he, personally, never showed up. He would even have Mother's Day cards sent to me. Over time they stopped, and we ceased to exist to him. I was alright with that, where I was concerned, because I didn't want anything from him. But our daughter, she didn't deserve that. Even after her trying to establish something with him years later, if she didn't reach out, he wouldn't. Finally, I said to her, "Stop and see what he does." To date, we haven't heard from him, and now, she doesn't want to see him at all. Only if he knew how amazing she was and how much she looks like him. My family teases me now that I'm being haunted by my exes. That's how much my children look like them. My cousin even says, if he wasn't there to see them delivered, he wouldn't think I was their mother. Good thing I'm not one of those crazy mothers who mistreats their kids out of anger towards their fathers. Nevertheless, him not seeing our daughter is one instance, still somehow it makes me feel rejected all over again.

In 2019, 14 years later, I made a trip back to the apartment we last lived in; the place I left and never looked back. I took my daughter there to show her where we lived but I could never call home. For her, it meant nothing. However, for me, it represented a place I broke free from physically but not emotionally. Sitting looking at the apartment door, I realized a part of me was still shut up in that house. My laughter stayed in that house. My belief in love stayed in that house. My stance as a woman stayed in that house. That day of my visit, I let that woman out. You, who's reading this, have a part of you that has been locked up some time ago. Maybe you have become so numb to life that you don't even feel a void inside. Maybe you have buried the past and hurts so much you don't even realize you are still bound by it. This is the moment right here, yes right here in this book, for you to be free. It was like the woman with an issue of blood. She dealt with her issue for 12 years. The bible says that in that time her situation didn't get any better, but it got worse. Then Jesus steps on the scene. I must jump to the part of the story that blesses me so much. The bible says, "When she heard." If you know the law of the time, it tells you that she couldn't be around people, she couldn't be married, she couldn't be around friends, she couldn't come to church, and she couldn't be loose around town. So, who did she have to talk to, for her to hear about Jesus? We all know the bible says, "Faith comes by hearing and hearing by the word of God." The bible also tells us "thy word I have hidden in my heart so that I may not sin against thee." It is the Word we have on the inside of us, that when we have no one around us, we still have it to pull from. That means for her, when she had no one, she still had the Word. I tell people all the time, when the preacher is not preaching, and the choir is not singing. When all I have is me and my situation, what do I have to lean on? I have the Word. I don't need a keyboard or a drum because I have the Word. It's the Word that keeps me. It's the Word that guides me. It's the Word that comforts me. In the midst of your chaos and confusion, I challenge you to pull on the Word. Isaiah shows us that it's the Word that sets captives free. I say again....BE FREE!

I mentioned to you after leaving him, I ran right into struggles. So much I could say about that. However, out of all I could say, there is one struggle worth mentioning. That is the struggle that came out of me not healing. By the natural eye, you would think it wasn't necessary, but in the spirit, I was all jacked up. I was too busy being what was necessary for my daughter, I never even considered myself. Such a repetitive cycle for me. I became numb to everything, that I didn't even know I was hurting. Somewhere along the way, I stopped living and was simply existing. One of the worst things we can do, and I mean a serious disservice, is to try and move on without healing. In Joshua 5, the Lord commanded Joshua and the people to circumcise themselves again. After which, the bible says, "They rest at a place they called Gilgal." After coming out of such a trying ordeal to get to the promise, it was necessary to heal themselves in preparation for the promise. Please know just because you came through a trying ordeal, does not mean you are not still entitled to your promise. But coming out of such a place, you can't just walk into your promise without first preparation. They had to circumcise, or trim away, those areas they can do without and those places where infection can reside. Trimming what you can do without is your willingness to let go to grow. It's like pruning your garden. For the new bloom to come forth, you must trim away the old. You're trimming away mindsets, possessions, people, whatever it will take to grow you out of that place. The whole journey for the children of Israel was a struggle because while trying to be free, their minds still had them bound. That is why they fell to false Gods and eventually died in the wilderness. They never dealt with their Egypt. So they never came to their promise. For many of us, the reason for the struggle to our promise is because we won't let go of Egypt. Many of us talk a game of freedom, but we are still living a shackled life. Might I admonish you? Don't die with your promise.

The second part of the definition, which in my eyes is the main part, is to trim away what can cause infection. This is the area we truly overlook. Coming out of a divorce, I never took time to examine my emotions. The types of emotions that commonly follow loss were things I was contending with unaware. That is until situations in my life caused them to spring forth. That's a dangerous place for anyone to be. I began lashing out at people and in places that didn't deserve this treatment. Hate, anger, sadness, depression, bitterness, loneliness, you name it all can take root and, if left untreated, can grow into something that will take over your life. I was happy leaving my ex-husband, but that doesn't mean I didn't need to heal. I endured a lot and before I moved on, I needed to close the door/the chapter. Many of you reading this, too, need to close the door/the chapter. You want to turn the page and experience the rest of the story, but you can't until you finish this current page. The bible says, "Old wine can't go into new wine skin or it will burst." That's because it doesn't have the capacity to hold what has expired. Don't allow your old to contend with your new. The biggest evidence that I didn't heal was the relationship I end up getting into. Yes, even after years had passed, I was still in the same place.

I thought my relationship with my ex-husband was interesting but honestly, this one took the cake. It's like I can, and I can't believe I got into it, all at the same time. Looking back, I believe I was bound to end up in a relationship like that. I can acknowledge it openly now, but this too used to be a secret shame. This man came into my life as a knight in shining armor; a powerful man of God, with a rich word. I initially didn't see the man because I held such respect and admiration for his gift and anointing. It was clear my pastor wasn't going to cultivate me in ministry. Yet, I knew, God chose me for something. It's hard to have a passion for ministry inside and no one there to cultivate it. This man truly came into my life at the right time and proved to be the wise counsel I needed. He never crossed the line nor did I. This was certainly contrary to what people thought, because they had already pegged me for a whore. I came to rationalize later; it wasn't solely based on the garbage said about me. It also stemmed from the man they knew him to be. How naïve I was at the time. I didn't want anything more from him than guidance and teaching. I had so many questions and so many dreams/visions I needed clarity on. Once again, true to form, I had no one to go to. He was there. Somewhere along our interaction, I started to carry him in my spirit. I prayed for him, his family and the ministry. I remember one afternoon, I was walking into work from lunch, and he dropped in my spirit so heavily. I picked up the phone, called and he answered. That day his voice didn't sound normal to me, but he assured all was okay. He was sitting at the park. A few years later, he admitted to me, the day I called, I stopped him from doing "something stupid" (his words). He was depressed and he was sitting at the park contemplating suicide, while getting drunk. Yes, this was the words of the preacher. Woe to you that believe we have it all together! That we don't struggle with emotions and dark thoughts. That we are above problems, pain and prayer. To the contrary, we need prayer, just as much, if not more. I can no longer count the times I have fallen into a depressed place and contemplated suicide. I was the preacher ministering deliverance over others' lives and not over her own. Anyway when I called, I shocked him back into reality. Moments like that I never take for granted. If God places someone on my heart, I reach out, even if they don't answer. I never know what the reason may be, but God knows. It's my prayer that when the Lord places me on someone's heart, they will respond the same. It would seem from the very beginning, we became knitted. We seem to love a lot of the same things, despite the age difference. One of the things I loved the most was our conversation. It wasn't just any conversation, but it was centered around the Word of God. We could bounce off each other revelation surrounding a text. We could help each other write a sermon sitting in the comforts of our living room. It was great. For that reason, it was hard for me to accept just how little I meant in his heart. Oh, I was a great impact in his life, but it never changed the place I carried in his heart. There were times I longed for him to drink just one too many because, it was then, he opened and let me in. I loved him so much and it was alright if he just liked me. Isn't it funny how we will give the full barrel to others but willingly accept the scrapings at the bottom in return? If you are like me, when you love, you love hard. There is never a question where your heart or your loyalty's lie. This is where I began developing my soul tie. What is a soul tie? Simply put, I would say it's an emotional bond that forms a deeper level of attachment. Sure, this word is not specifically stated in the bible but there are numerous accounts that speak to it. These are connections, happening between two people, that are normally unhealthy in nature. There are soul ties that are deemed healthy, as in marriage. In this instance, this tie was detrimental to my life. I, like so many others, don't even realize you are dealing with a soul tie, until you are wrapped up in it. It's sad to say this but he became an addiction for me. That is a key sign that you are dealing with a soul tie, when your affection to them becomes an addiction for you.

While incarcerated, I spent my time amongst people who struggled with a drug addiction. Can I tell you right here, we all have dealt with an addiction, just in different forms? Mine is to shoes and I'm still battling with that monkey (smile). While locked up, in the groups we had to attend, there was a key lesson I learned. The reason why so many addicted to drugs overdose is because they are chasing their first high. The part they seem to ignore is that they will never get that high again. Their body has started to develop a tolerance that won't allow them to go back. So, they take more and more and more, hoping to achieve it, to find they fail. I thought about that when it came to my affections towards this man. Every time we were together, I desired for it to be like the first time. Every smile he would give me; I would want it to be like the first time. Every time he would caress my hand, I would hope that it would be like the first time. It became so sad that I would do things to recreate the atmosphere that would lead to the first time. Just like that addict, I was doping up the equation hoping to come to the solution, and in the end I would fail. Sure, there were nights I would get him to have sex with me, but I still failed because I never won his heart. It's taken me so long to write this book because of this very part I'm sharing with you. This is as naked as it will get because this was the lowest I've been in my life. No, incarceration was not my lowest. This was.

I remember the day he arrived in my city. He was going through a divorce and life, in general, was dealing him a really bad hand. Just as it seemed the light was starting to shine again, the rug got pulled from under him again. The reasoning for his arrival to the city was to pastor a church. Upon his arrival, he never heard from the pastor and he really had no place to go. At that time, I had a place of my own and would have been more than happy to make room for him. However, my mom made the decision to open her home to him. To this day, she asks herself, what was she thinking opening her home. She didn't know this strange man and she just let him live with her. He looked so pitiful at the time, who could say no? And just like that, we became what he needed. I used to think often back on those beginning moments and questioned, *why was it again he didn't love me?* Didn't he at least feel that he owed me? I made life way too convenient for him. Everything he wanted and needed was right at his hand. I would even give him money out of my paycheck before I tithed. I was caught all the way up. 2 Peter 2:19b NLT, "For you are a slave to whatever controls you." Remember I told you that, for some of us, we don't even know we are contending with a soul tie until we are all wrapped up into one. I remember the day when I came to that revelation. This is a day that's so etched into my mind, I'm still uncomfortable with checking voicemails. While living with us, he discovered he was under some legal scrutiny. It wasn't just a minor legal battle but one that was after taking his life. He sought spiritual counsel, legal counsel and he concluded he would just face it. Before he could face it, the authorities made him do it. I was at work and I had just gotten off the phone with him. I stepped away from my desk and when I came back, I saw I missed a call from him, and he had left me a voicemail message. That was unlike him and what was even more unusual, I decided to check it. The sound on the voicemail was so chaotic. It was the authorities banging on the door for him to come out. What a nightmare!! Someone please wake me up now, was all I could say inside. I panicked! I called my mom and she already knew because they had reached out to her. Well I lost it. I started hyper ventilating uncontrollably, to the point, the ambulance was called, and off to the hospital I went. My soul had been so tied into him, that I almost lost my life. LITERALLY! Needless to say, it was truly an uphill legal battle for him but, in the end, he won. Before you ask, the details surrounding his case are for him to tell. I know you want to be nosey (smile). I will tell you though, it wasn't a hill he climbed alone. It got to the place, each of my free moments was spent eating, sleeping, and breathing his case. So, when I got into trouble, I just knew he would be there for me. I was wrong, Wrong, WRONG! You know what though? All is well. It took me a long time to be able to say that, but today I can. I'm proud of that.

Coming out of that relationship, you would have thought that I learned what not to do in my next. Truthfully, my choices after would say I have not. Married men certainly weren't the answer, but here I go. I'm sure you are like, well duh of course not, they are married. Actually, that didn't bother me. To the contrary, I liked that aspect because it left me with no attachments. True to form, I enjoyed being the mistress because I could get spoiled and never had to bring anyone home. I sound awful, don't I? When you have such a hole in your heart, you will try to do anything to fill it. To include, filling it with lies you tell yourself. Sure, I said I wanted no attachments, but no one clued my heart into that. Here I was again, secretly in love and no one loved me back. Sure, he said he did but if he loved me, he would be with me right? Once again I'm left holding a bag of words and emotions. Serves me right I would say. Getting involved in something like that was wrong and dangerous. Why should I be okay with doing that to myself? I deserve to give my time, attention and affection to someone that can cherish it and give it back. Here I was in my recurring trap...something felt better than nothing. One of the other poor decisions I ended up finding myself making is gravitating to who I believed was a prophecy come true. I don't know about you but I have so much prophecy my cup, plate and cabinet are overflowing. I remember one year I was prophesied to more than 17 times about getting married. I stop counting at that point and if someone spoke anything close to marriage, I tuned them out. Somewhere along the way, the words resonated with me and became a daily thought for me. Could it be, me married? Is this really about to come true? I'm going to have a father for my kids? All of those thoughts flowed through my mind. So much so, when it looked like it, I thought this was it. I didn't inspect to see if it walked like it, quacked like it, sounded like it. I just decided this was it. One of the most dangerous things we can do is manipulate our prophecy. We never allow God to fulfill His words. Instead, we make it happen for Him. In doing this, we need to realize we are cheating ourselves out of possibly ever coming to see who/what God has for us. Here is the realization. God does not need our help. I know you may not believe this, but everyone is not prophesying. Some are prophelying. Because we desire so much, we miss this because we turn our discernment way down. Then when it doesn't work, we get mad with God. Maybe that's not your story, but it certainly was mine. Whenever we get a word, no matter who it's from, we must discern if what we're hearing is from God. That is so important. Once you find that out, then you need to know if it's a word for now or later. In the bible, David was anointed king years before he took the throne. Just because he was anointed does not mean it was his appointed time. We don't like to wait. This is a microwave era. Fast and quick is how we want it. How unfortunate it is we forget good things do come to those who wait. May I remind you? What God has for you, is for you. No one can take that from you. That's something I tell myself daily. I also had to remind myself single does not equal desperate. Singles have a bad rep but for a great deal, it's one that is earned. The way we carry ourselves and our behaviors make others draw that conclusion of us. Where I am today, I never want anyone to think that of me. Nor do I want them to misunderstand my "ready" for desperation. Never portray yourself in such a way that they confuse your "ready" with desperation. Sure you are ready to love but not just anyone. Sure you are ready to be committed but not to be treated like crap. There is a standard but no one will ever know it if you never set it and make them adhere to it. Alone doesn't mean lonely. Not everyone deserves your company. Trust me, this list I could keep going with, but I will leave it with a repeat. Never let your "ready" come across as desperation. Many days I was desperate, but not anymore. I already know I'm not the only person that's been in this place. It's hard but I want my wounds to bring you healing. If for nothing else I need you to know, you matter. I know I said the details of my ex's story belongs to him, but there is one little detail I must tell. In the midst of his battle, I got pregnant with our son.

This will take courage and a whole lot of honesty, but I want you to think about Soul Ties and the ones' you contend(ed) with. How do I know you ask? Allow me to use a scripture reference to pull that out. The bible says in John 15:5, "I am the vine, you are the branches. He who abides in Me, and I in him, bears much fruit; for without Me you can do nothing."

Using this verse, we can identify:

1. *It's something that disconnects us from God.*
2. *It's something we can't pull life from. It brings death.*
3. *It's something that causes us to stop bearing fruit but reap frustration, emotionally and spiritually.*

4. It's something that blinds us to our state of bondage. We lose sight we are doing nothing because our focus is solely on the tie.

I hoped that helped. Now what I desire for you to do is write your ties. One of the first important things to overcoming your tie is acknowledging you have one. Once you write them down, then I want you to pray for release from them. Our God is a deliverer and He is the Lord that delivers us from all. Only if we want it.

_____

_____

_____

_____

_____

_____

_____

_____

_____

_____

_____

_____

_____

How Do I Break My Soul Tie?

The first thing you need to realize is God loves you. We have a tendency to disqualify ourselves from Gods love because of the things we've done and the places we've been. The bible tells us that nothing can separate us from the love of God. Despite our wrongs and our mess, God loves us. A lot of times we find ourselves in the ties that bind because of the lack of love we feel. Right now, let me tell your heart, God loves you. Second, please accept forgiveness. But the initial forgiveness is the forgiveness from God. Ephesians 1:7, "In Him we have redemption through his blood, the forgiveness of sins in accordance with the riches of God's grace that he lavished on us." Ephesians 4:32 ESV, "Be kind to one another, tenderhearted, forgiving one another, as God in Christ forgave you." Remember Calvary, a place where Jesus gave of His life for the forgiveness of our sins. God loves you and He forgives you. This is key in breaking a tie, trusting that our God is a redeeming God.

The second forgiveness, and this is so important, forgive yourself. To this day, I am still having a hard time forgiving myself for some things. Not necessarily what I did to me, but what my actions caused for someone else. There are some things right now that you hang your head in shame over. You don't need anyone else to criticize you because you do a good job by yourself. You must forgive yourself. Romans reminds us that all have sinned and come short of the glory of God. In the story of the woman caught in the act of adultery, the people brought her to Jesus. They told him what was customary for them to do to her and in response, Jesus knelt and wrote in the sand. He rose and said to them, "He who is without sin cast the first stone," and he began to write again. As he was writing, those there to stone her, left one by one. The only one that can hold you to your past, issues, and mistakes, is you. Forgive yourself.

Third, confess. Above this I had you write out your soul ties and then pray a Prayer of Release. The act of praying openly says, "God, I acknowledge there is a tie and I admit I can't do this by myself." The bible teaches us that if we confess ours sins, God is faithful to forgive. There goes that word again, *forgiveness*. You must realize just how important that part is. It was the allowing of something to take residence inside that caused you to arrive at this place. Replacing it with someone/something doesn't always repair, but it will keep you in the very place you desire to be free from.

Lastly, keep praying. It's so important to yield to the voice of God. He won't speak if you don't welcome Him to talk. When you pray to Him, in turn God will commune with you. The posture of prayer, that released you from the tie, is the same you will need to stay free. It is just like the saying for a relationship...*What it took to get them is the same needed to keep them.* What it took to get your relationship with God, is the same effort and more you will need to keep it. The bible teaches to pray without ceasing. Below, I have left space for you to write your own Prayer of Release. There is no format. Just be honest with yourself. Then make this prayer a part of your day to day. Add to it or change it completely if necessary. Just make this your moment to break free.

Prayer of Release

Allow me to leave you with one more nugget concerning soul ties:

1. Stay away from potential temptation. Allowing it in your space can cause you to fall subject to it. Relapse is real!
2. Put a guard on your thoughts and your heart.
3. Stay in your Word to be governed by it.
4. Live a life pleasing unto God.
5. Do not compromise.

Because we live in a world that has changed so much, it's easy to fall into temptation. It is easy to be swayed by the things one should not approve of. We are called to be in the world, but not of the world. Might I encourage you with this:

"No temptation has overtaken you except such as is common to man; but God is faithful, who will not allow you to be tempted beyond what you are able, but with the temptation will also make the way of escape, that you may be able to bear it."

1 Corinthians 10:13

"Stand therefore, having girded your waist with truth,
having put on the breastplate of righteousness, and
having shod your feet with the preparation of the gospel
of peace; above all, taking the shield of faith with which
you will be able to quench all the fiery darts of the
wicked one. And take the helmet of salvation, and the
sword of the Spirit, which is the word of God; praying
always with all prayer and supplication in the Spirit..."
Ephesians 6:14-18a

1. Gird yourself with truth. We find truth in God and we stay connected to that truth by the Word of God.

2. Breastplate: protect your hearts and adorn yourself with His righteousness. Isaiah 61:10 NKJV, "I will greatly rejoice in the Lord, My soul shall be joyful in my God; For He has clothed me with his garments of salvation, He has covered me with the robe of righteousness, As a bridegroom decks himself with ornaments, And as a bride adorns herself with her jewels."

3. Walk in peace. Wherever we go, walk in peace and represent our Lord, who is our peace (Shalom).

4. Your faith will shield you from the fiery darts the enemy will throw your way. Your belief in God and standing on what He can do will keep you from falling to the temptation of the enemy.

5. Helmet your head with salvation: remember that it was He that saved you. Keeping that thought in mind will keep the enemy from using death against you. He came that we might have life. I said to you before when I struggled with living, I remember that He gave His life so I may live. If I didn't matter, then why would He do that?

6. Carry your sword every day. If you forget any other piece, never go without the Word. Every time the Lord was tempted by the enemy, He replied to him, "It is written." Remember what God spoke concerning you. It is written in the heavens. When the enemy comes against you, speak the Word back at him. God's Word has not changed concerning you.

I ended the verse with something that is so important and that is prayer. I begin and end everything in prayer. Its His voice that guides me and it's His that should guide you. Keeping tuned into His voice will hinder access for any other. John 10:4-5 KJV, "And when he putteth forth his own sheep, he goeth before them, and the sheep follow him: for they know his voice. And a stranger will they not follow, but will flee from him: for they know not the voice of strangers."

FREEDOM IN A BOUND PLACE

"Bad things do happen; how I respond to them defines my character and the quality of my life. I can choose to sit in perpetual sadness, immobilized by the gravity of my loss, or I can choose to rise from the pain and treasure the most precious gift I have – life itself."

~Walter Anderson

Being pregnant with my son brought me so much joy. The fact that he was conceived out of wedlock never stopped me from loving each kick and late-night snack attack I experienced. Even my doctor exclaimed how delightful and to the text book my pregnancy was. That was certainly a difference from my first one, because with my daughter, I stayed sick and even went into labor early. I should have taken that as a sign of how she would be now. She does things all in her time. It makes me so mad at times but isn't that teenagers. It is my prayer, that in time, that will change. She has dreams as high as the galaxy and I want her to shoot for them all. My son is truly the delight of our family. We call him Charlie and we are his angels (my mom, daughter and I). With all the joy that I feel, it doesn't take away the tears shed in the process. I knew the exact day I conceived my son. It's funny how a woman can become so in tuned with her body, that she can determine something like that. I could and I did. I remember the look on his dad's face when I told him, considering it was only a few days after we were intimate with each other. I told him then "I'm having your son, with or without you." We had already had a scare before, and I remember what it felt like to have an abortion in the past. With that said, I knew I was never doing that again. While I spoke with such strength to him concerning my decision, I was shaking on the inside. I was scared because I didn't want to raise this baby by myself. Honestly, I didn't want to become someone else's baby momma. I wanted him to love me and we be a family. I didn't want to just share our son and we do the visitation thing. No, I wanted him at home with me and we live our lives together. I didn't get pregnant to keep him, but I must be honest, I hoped it would make him stay.

During my pregnancy, he was wonderful. I've always heard "happy wife, happy life". Well, I wasn't his wife, but he made me so happy, to where we lived a happy life. We traveled together and the bigger I got, the more attentive he became. It got to the point he never left my side. I was in heaven. This was the exact attention I wanted and deserved. Now looking back, I do wonder what was his reasoning for doing all that he did. I was so blinded by getting what I wanted, that I never stopped to ask was it really what I needed. Have you ever experienced a point in your life like that? You want something so bad that you fail to see that it's not something you really need. Yeah, he was attentive to me, and all the other women he dealt with. While he was dealing with his legal battle, I had hoped my being there would open his eyes to who was really there for him. I remember, when it first began, he gave me a list of people to contact because he was so confident they would support. Without me even telling you, I ask, how many of them do you really think did? We are all guilty of that, aren't we? We have our list of people that we believe will be there for us. Yep, whatever the reasoning may be, you are so certain that if called, they will answer. Then when they don't, we find ourselves so crushed. I've come to learn to stop seeking approval from people God never approved for my life. I said it earlier, I really had hoped his heart would change towards me. The question is "why buy the cow when you can get the milk for free"?

This makes me think about the Leah and Rachel story. If I was to be a character, of course, I would be Leah, the overlooked and unloved one. Oh, you know the story. She is the daughter, that after years of servitude, was given to Jacob when Laban tricked him. She wasn't the one Jacob chose but was made to be his choice. The bible illustrates so clearly for us the love Jacob had for Rachel. Yet, it also shows us the sons that he conceived with Leah. Do you know how hard that must have been for Leah to give of herself to someone that didn't give it back? And with each child she bore, she hoped...

The son, *Reuben:* "The Lord has noticed my misery, and now my husband will love me." The sadness her heart must have felt to lay beside a man that probably couldn't stand her. The bible tells us that she wasn't easy on the eyes. During this time, daughters were traded by their fathers in business deals. I'm sure it was Rachel who the father used. The one that was the center of everyone's attention. It must be miserable to be in a family and go unnoticed and now to be married and still no one sees you. There are times that I have felt this way; unnoticed. As I said at the beginning, you are surround by tons of people and still feel alone. There are times we find ourselves doing things in hopes it will cause us to be seen or to be valued.

The son, *Simeon*: "The Lord heard that I was unloved and has given me another son." Not only is she not seen, but inside she feels unloved. The truth is, she really wasn't loved by the man she gave herself to. One of the things I dealt with was lying beside a man who I knew didn't love me as much as I loved him. I think about the nights when a particular woman would call him and he would take the call right then, with me laying in his arms. He would tell her things, and, in my head, I would be like, *she is so dumb*. The reality is, I was the dumb one. How could I let him do that to me? I remember when I took him away for his birthday and while gone, he got sick. So, I spent the trip taking care of him and that was no easy task. And

101

while driving back, his phone kept ringing and it was one woman after another. There were so many other instances I allowed him to put women in my face. With each one I took it with a smile and convinced myself repeatedly that it didn't bother me. Who was I kidding though?

The son, *Levi*: "Surely this time my husband will feel affection for me, since I have given him three sons!" This point she felt after I've done all and endured all, this must be the icing that will change his heart and his mind. How wrong she was? There are times we have given everything we have to give. Blood, sweat, and tears and it still never seems to be enough. We convince ourselves that at this point, we have done all that's necessary. Every qualification they have, I must have met by now. To find, at the end of the day, enough is never enough. I always felt, the day I almost lost my life would be enough. To this day, it's still not enough. For many, you may think I'm angry and this is a bitter place. Can I tell you just how free and happy I am? Let me say it in the last one.

The son, *Judah*: "Now I will praise the Lord." Here is the answer to how free and happy I am. There comes a point in our lives where the limit is reached and crossed. It takes some of us to be crushed before we realize this place. I want to talk to that one like I had to talk to myself. Yes, it may seem it took you a long time to get here, but the blessing is you have arrived. I always beat myself up on how long it took for the lights to come on. Not today. I'm just glad that I grew from that place instead of dying in that place. Sure, our hearts were hurt but that's because we love so hard. We give of our everything and there should never be a moment we regret the heart God gave us. It's just we faltered in knowing who to give it to. But just like Leah, we come to a place where we wise up and we give God the praise. I made it through misery; I made it through being unloved. I even made it through giving of my very last and for that reason, I give God the praise.

While you may be looking at the children in a natural sense, the birthing speaks so much more than that. It did for me at least. I birthed out my Reuben. I birthed my Simeon and I finally got to the place where I birthed out my Levi. It happened 16 days after my son was born. My legal troubles had started way before 2012, but this particular year the roosters came home to roost. I had received a letter that I needed to be present in court. It was a routine that I was accustomed to, but for some reason this didn't feel the same. I had this awful feeling inside and the closer the court date approached, the more in knots my stomach became. Everything within me told me this time when I went to court, I wasn't coming home anytime soon. At the time, my daughter was in elementary school, my mom was recently out of work and the father of my son wasn't working. I got up early that morning and so many things came to mind. The first being what got me in this mess in the first place. I use to work at a branch of a bank that needed some help getting organized. I should've known then it was a ship that was bound to sink. Who would have known its sinking would come at a point when I was doing wrong? Financially, things became extremely hard for me. Before separating from my ex-husband, he had depleted all my bank accounts. Shortly after leaving him, the bill collectors came knocking. They weren't even my bills, but because I was attached to his name, that made me just as liable. Who came up with those rules I wondered? Before I knew it, the garnishments started kicking in. It just became a convenient thought to take a little money here and a little money there. The devil knew just what button to press to get me to go forward with the thought.

James 1:14-15 NLT, "Temptation comes from our own desires, which entice us and drag us away. These desires give birth to sinful actions. And when sin is allowed to grow, it gives birth to death." That day, and everyone after, is such a blur to me. It's almost like I blacked out. The enemy had control over me, because I gave in to my own desires, but how many of you know God will provide a way of escape? It took a totally separate incident to break me free. I already told you the branch I worked at needed some help. We had our routine audit and it was found that we were out of compliance. Well, as the old saying goes, "The captain goes down with the ship." I was told I was fired and there was nothing I could do about it. I had a fit and not for the reason you think. My mind wasn't on the loss of income. My mind was they were going to find out the crime I had been committing. My heart breaks now typing this because I was the one that jumped at the sight of a cop car. I drove under the speed limit and obeyed all traffic signs. What happened to me? People truly underestimate the powers we wrestle against. Ephesians 6:12 KJV says, "For we wrestle not against flesh and blood, but against principalities, against powers, against the rulers of the darkness of this world, against spiritual wickedness in high places." It is so important to stay prayed up and to keep your gates guarded. We must be careful with what we see, what we hear, what we think and so forth. You must know eventually what you take in, will come back out. The more I contemplated the action, it's no surprise I lived it out. I was fighting a spiritual battle that I allowed to happen because I left my gate open (my mind). Once I lost my job, the ball rolled from there.

The extension of what I was accused of was found not to be my fault, but I wasn't completely without fault. Before long, I was standing before a judge awaiting to hear my fate. I will never forget the first go round of this legal battle, that morning the prosecuting attorney looked at me and I could see he was thinking. It was once the proceedings began that I realized his thoughts were to set me free. No one in my position had ever just gone home but that day I did. I was so grateful to God that I passed out on my way out of the court room. But how many of you caught where I said my first go around?

Well, from the beginning until 2012, I fought to keep my freedom. Somewhere along the way, my sight became clouded again. No, I wasn't doing the same thing that got me into trouble the first time, but I did fail to guard my gate. There I was again wrestling another spiritual battle. I stopped caring about myself because I made someone else my world and in the end, I paid the price. The morning I was summonsed to court, I kissed my daughter and told her that I would be waiting for her at the bus stop when she got out of school. I didn't have the heart to tell my daughter you may not see mommy for a while. I went back home, and I looked in on my mom and I kissed her. I went to my son's room and I cradled him in my arms. I placed him against my face, and I took a whiff of his sweet-smelling skin. I rocked him and kissed him. I wanted to hold on to that minute because I felt it would be my last for a while. I wanted my son to feel my heartbeat once more. How I wished he could see my face, but he was so young I knew that was impossible. I didn't want him to forget about me or think another woman was his mother. Lastly, I went into the room where my son's father lay, and I told him I was leaving. He jumped up because he wanted to go with me to court that day. I couldn't bear him going with me either. I told him no and that I wanted to go alone. That I would take care of it and be right back. I said to him, "Stay and take care of the baby. Don't worry about me." Sitting here today, I wonder if I had let him go, would things have turned out different.

That morning when I got to court, I had no one speaking for me. The judge I had, all those years, retired. My attorney met with the new prosecutor and he quit on me. I didn't know at the time I was entitled to a continuance when that happens. I had the right to have legal counsel, but he never told the court that he dropped me. I never understood the dynamics of what was happening that day. But moments after my case was called, I was being taken away in handcuffs, facing two years. Who was going to take care of my family? Who was going to nurse my newborn baby? Who was going to take care of my mother's heart that I know was breaking? How did I let this happen to me? All the years of hard work and good behavior were destroyed in one blink of an eye. Matthew 5:29-30 NLT says, "So if your eye – even your good eye – causes you to lust, gouge it out and throw it away. It is better for you to lose one part of your body than for your whole body to be thrown into hell. And if your hand – even your stronger hand – causes you to sin, cut it off and throw it away. It is better for you to lose one part of your body than for your whole body to be thrown into hell." When I first read this scripture, I never really understood what it meant until now. Jesus was telling us it's better to deal with that one area before it spreads and becomes a total infection. It's like leaving an argument unresolved. Where you had one incident to address, but when left, it can fester into an overall dislike or even hate you now must overcome. I was famous for leaving loose ends in my life. It was better for me to act as if it didn't exist instead of facing and addressing them. What I should have cut off, or dealt with a long time ago, I never did and now look where it had gotten me. It is believed facing things can cause a lot of pain. Truth is, not facing them to me, brings so much more. Jesus knew that, and His Word admonishes us, do not do it. I have to say this, as I've said before, what should have been the worst time of my life, end up being the best. How could that be possible you ask? My time away was meant for me to separate from things that were killing me. My mindset, behaviors, relationships and more, were taking the very life from me. I didn't find God while there because I already had Him. However, the relationship I was supposed to have with Him, I did find. I came to find the me that wasn't existing based on people pleasing or molding into some person I thought I needed to be. I wasn't looking for applause anymore, although I got it. This applause was true celebration, not just people's toleration. I came to see just how toxic the relationship my son's father and I had. He had such a self-centered mentality. All the sacrifices I made for him and he couldn't even make a fraction for me. I remember the time this became very clear for me. Being away from my children was very hard for me. It was even harder because one of my children was a newborn. I remember my son's father got an assignment away in New York, or so he told me. From the very beginning, he tried to convince me that our son was going to be with him. He was so emphatic about it that he made me feel bad for asking. He said that I made him feel unfit as a father. No matter what he said, something inside of me just didn't feel right about it. The trip went and came to an end and it seemed I was possibly wrong. Everything seemed to go well until I got on the phone with a friend. While on the phone with them, they wanted to thank me for allowing them to keep my infant son. I played it off and I thanked them for being willing to keep him for us. Every second after that, all I could see was red. I asked her to hand the phone to him and the moment he came on the phone, I let him have it. To this day, I don't even believe he understands. It wasn't about him lying, oh because that is awful. My anger came from why would he do that to me while I was in prison. He knew what it was like to be behind bars. It wasn't that long ago he was in my place. However, he didn't have to do it with a child out here. I did and he would put my spirit and heart through that. Inside I knew something was wrong from the jump. That wouldn't be the last time he did things, with our son, that would make me stress out. I shed so many tears over this man, it got to the place I became numb. It was one night, after hanging up with him, that I sat in my dark cell with tears in my eyes. I looked over at a watch he bought me for Christmas prior to me leaving, and I realized the battery had died. Immediately that spoke to me. It was time for me to let whatever we had die. It sounds crazy, but that night saved me. It was necessary for me to go through what I did there, because every awful thing he did before didn't seem to wake me up. It was like I knew this was wrong but I kept hoping. Now, all the wanting that I had for him to be better, casually faded away and it didn't matter anymore. Just as Leah, in time, I gave God the praise. God kept me through all my mess, and He blessed me. The things I were able to do while incarcerated and the things I had a hand in seeing come to pass. The things established and the lives that were touched. Who God always destined me to be started to blossom forth. Yes, right behind bars. I became free in my bound place.

Please know every day was not a sunny day. There were plenty of trials along the way. With each day though, I could see more and more of God's plan He had for my life. Can I tell you sometimes your hardest place will be your blessed place? I told you that after all Joseph endured, he rose to a place of great authority and prosperity. Even when he birthed two sons, their names carried a meaning of victory in Joseph's life. His first son was named Manasseh, meaning "God has made me forget all my troubles and everyone in my father's family." What you saw as my bound place, became my birthing place. I was freed from the troubles of my past and the hurts I held from my family. The first place I experienced rejection no longer had control over my heart or mind. Can I release that over your life too? Oh, I came to make the devil real mad with this book. Your family issues will no longer hold control over your heart or mind. Whatever your mother did or whatever your father did does not matter. Your fight may have been with your sister or brother. Today I don't care where the trouble in your family lies, God said that He is birthing you out of that place. This season of your life you are set free. The troubles that settled in your past, that try to haunt your present, God says you are free. Your mistakes, shortcomings, faults, struggles, tears, fears, closed doors, walkaways, back stabs, and I could go on. God said every one of those troubles you are free. This moment He is birthing you out of your misery. He is birthing you out of your shame. When God disconnected me, He was using that to reattach me to the place I needed to be. You may not recognize why things happen as they do in your life, but may you consider this? It was God who sent the disconnect so that He could reconnect you to your rightful place. I didn't understand at first why the lockup, but can I tell you the behaviors that got me into trouble years ago, were the same behaviors that stayed with me. Sure, I may have not done the same things, but my mindset hadn't changed. God had to separate me. It isn't promised to feel good, but the promise is it shall work for our good. The name of Joseph's second son is Ephraim, meaning "God has made me fruitful in this land of my grief." My God, I told you that your hardest place shall be your blessed place. God has destined for your very enemies to bless you. Those that tried to stop you and take from you, are the very ones God said He will raise to bless you. After the divorce, where others died and gave up, you shall live and be blessed. I didn't die in my situation. Someone had to live to tell the story. Don't you know that? The truth of the story had to be told. That's why we're still here.

After I was released, people started coming back and apologizing to me. I didn't run them away because God told me they would come. There are those that will come back that owe you an apology. They came to know their lives would never move forward until they went back and made it right. Just as Samuel told Jesse and his boys when it came to David, no one can sit until he comes. There were tables they never got to set because of the ones they kept you from. There were doors never opened unto them because of the ones they shut in your face. God says the place that tried to afflict you is the place God has assigned to now bless you. We must be careful not to run or move too soon. It may have hurt, but it came back to heal.

There was so much I learned while being locked up that I couldn't even express it all within these pages. I will say though there was a strength I obtained that I never knew lied within me. I stood up for myself like I never had before. At times, I felt bad about it but for the most part, I was proud of the woman I was becoming. Real ministry began for me behind those walls. I know many say that it's not real because its religion out of convenience. But I told you, I already knew about God. I was preaching before I got locked up. For me, it wasn't a convenience but it was a conviction. I finally came to a place where I didn't just want to minister it to others. I wanted to live it for myself. I helped to license people in ministry while locked up. Yes, I did! I assisted with re-establishing the choir. I even got a chance to do something that was never done at the jail and, I believe has never been done again. Women weren't allowed to look or socialize with the men. Easter Sunday, we had a guest church come to the jail and the entire campus was invited. The women went in first, so that all of the men could sit behind. During the program, I got so wrapped up into it, I thought I had gotten myself into trouble. The Sergeant called me over and I just knew I was going on lock down. In actuality, they were asking if I would sing for them and I said, "Yes!" In order to sing, I had to stand in front of them. Remember, I said we weren't allowed to look at the men, but I did that day. As a matter of fact, I got a clear picture of everyone who was there that day. Every ranking official, to include the

Sheriff, was there. I sang my heart out and ministered to everyone there. There was not one dry eye in the building. No matter where I was, I was still who God says I am. That day I hold dear to my heart. I learned so much while I was there. I get mad at myself from time to time because I felt I cheated myself out of so much by coming into life lessons so late. There are days now I struggle because of the choices of my past, that I know I should have never made. But instead of allowing them to bind or break me, I use them to build me. I'm sure there are days you face with tear filled eyes because you too hate the choices you made. Might I comfort your heart as God did mine? All of this is for your making. There is a place of freedom we all must strive to get to. The place where the devil can no longer control us with the things of our past. He can't disrupt our present dreams with nightmares and fears. He can't make us feel unworthy because of mistakes and shortcomings. The bible tells us "whom the son sets free is free indeed." This freedom no one or nothing can take from you. There is a place of joy and peace that no one can take from you. Come to a place where you say, "I will not let this rob me anymore. I will not give it away anymore. I will not allow unnecessary access anymore."

The quote at the beginning said, 'I could focus on all that has happened to me or I can rise above it and cherish the greatest gift given to me, and that is life." I choose life today. It was a long, hard road and still is today. One that still comes with struggles, but I still choose it today. Some days I still have tears and regrets, and I wouldn't take nothing for them. There is no other choice for me. Today choose life. There is a beautiful present that will rise out of the ashes of your past. There is a place of fulfillment and peace just waiting for you. It's certainly something that is not impossible, but one that does come with a choice. Choose life.

MISUNDERSTOOD IN MINISTRY

"You do not have to be unusually gifted to make a difference in our world. You just have to be brave enough to allow God to use your gifts unusually well."

~Unknown~

his is one chapter that won't be as long as the others because it's one that I'm still writing. Ministry is not something that I do but it is who I am. From childhood, I knew the Lord called me to do something in the kingdom. At first, I didn't have a clear picture of it and honestly, to this day, I still don't. There is a great joy that I have in it unfolding but I must tell you, there are more days I wonder if this is what I'm supposed to do. From the very beginning, it seemed no one wanted me to do ministry. I know for those on the outside, you would say, that is the indication that you are on the right track. Tell that to my heart which hurt after countless disappointments. Or after every time I tried to serve and either the pastor would try me or his wife, because she thought I wanted him. I already told you that people in the church has a preconceived notion about me, and what's sad is that I grew up around them. Being thought the worst hurts more than being talked about. Sounds strange, but it does. There is so much more I could say but this is what I want to say. I took all of that, and in time, I have used it to grow my ministry. I know of the misunderstanding ministry can bring; therefore, God has allowed me to bring back hope and clarity of what God intended it to be. It takes a special grace, as I said, to share the ugly of your life and it brings beauty to another. I am alright with being that one. I want that young one to know they are special just as they are. That being called at a young age is not wrong. That being used after a divorce is not wrong. Being chosen by God after living in sin is not wrong. I remember when I separated from my ex-husband, I came back to my home church. I had been licensed as an evangelist when married and I wanted to continue to grow in God. It is funny how the pastor in that church saw more in me than the pastor of my home church. Maybe he did see it, but he didn't want to do anything with it. I dare not point fingers but it's a fact, for many of us, that some will never help us because they are afraid we will become greater than them. Even if they aren't worried about you being greater, they don't want the spotlight to come off them. Nevertheless, I came back in hopes of growing, to experience yet another period of rejection. After doing all that was asked of me, I got to the week of my initial sermon, to never see it come to pass. The day of, I had a meeting with the pastor, and he felt my giving wasn't adequate enough. You know this is really my first time talking about this. I always felt like if I said anything, I would be making myself look bad. When in truth, by never saying anything all these years allowed people to believe what they wanted and that became the truth. I never could understand why he would say that I didn't give, when every Sunday I gave. It may have not always been as much as I had wanted or even what it should. When I first got back home, I met with the pastor for counseling. I had just left my husband and I was struggling. I mentioned earlier about my financial bind. I would think that my pastor would have understood, but to my misfortune, he didn't. Instead he took my struggle and used it against me.

For years, I've tried to convince myself otherwise and I just can't. Many that grew up in church with me, ask me now, why I don't really come back or have anything to do with him. I want to tell them so bad sometimes, but I don't because it doesn't matter anymore. I guess if they want to know now, they can read the book. That Sunday he took my light away from me. He told me the day of he couldn't license me because he didn't want my ministry to start off like that. It would show I had a faith issue. How could he determine where my level of faith was? I was walking solely in faith because I was losing left and right, with a small child who didn't ask to be here, while living in my parents' home. It was each day that I lived by faith, that God would lead me and keep me. My heart and my mind, He sheltered me from the destruction of the storms. At that point, my faith dwindled because I wondered how God could let something like that happen to me. I didn't ask God that when I could have been molested. I didn't ask God that when I went through that awful marriage. I didn't ask God that when my son's father dogged me. I didn't even ask that when I had my home stolen right from under me or even when I was put in jail. No, it wasn't any of those times, but that time I did wonder.

I wanted more than anything to serve God. That morning, I sat across from the pastor and couldn't believe the words that were coming out of his mouth. I walked out of that office, refusing to let him see me cry, and I never looked back. When I left that day, I didn't just leave the church, but I left God. No wonder I ran into the devil's arms. There are so many of us out here that have been hurt by one leader or another. They go about without even giving a thought to our hearts, as if we don't have one. They step on us and discard us as if we're trash. Today, I'm not mad at him nor even hurt anymore. I think of what that day meant for me and I promised God, if He ever put me in a place where my voice would ever matter, I would minister to the hearts of His people to keep them from ending up like me. Sure, people think it's not so bad for me, but it really is. I have a hard time trusting and believing in the people I preach to. They say they love me, but that word has come with such disappointment that I don't know how to receive. It was lately I had someone come in the image of a friend and then end up being a foe; a true opportunist, out for self at my expense. It got hard writing this page, but my son walked up and said, "These are the last words, Mommy. You can do this."

If you could see my face right now, you would see my tears because God is freeing my heart. I minister the way I do because I know the delivering power of God. How His forgiveness is nothing like man could ever give. That His compassion and love is unfailing. We say, "Great is thy faithfulness," but it really is great.

I have been doing ministry since I was eight years old. I was supposed to give a speech, during Youth Sunday on violence. Somehow my speech turned into a sermon and from that day forth I was sold out. I went years being handed around as a rag because the pastor didn't want me and he blackballed me from others helping me. I was treated like I was a thing. I finally got licensed because a pastor stood up for me but that too was temporary. I then found myself in a safe place. That's how I met my son's father. The pastor of that church was radical just like me and had no problems calling out my mess. She saw who God anointed me to be, even after calling me a wild ass. Oh, and I miss her presence because when she left, so did my security. To date, I'm still kind of out here alone. I have a leader, but I never wanted one by name alone. I wanted someone who I could sit under and learn. One that could pour into me and spend time pruning me. Lord knows I need it. It's alright today because I see that's not God's full plan for me. There is such a strength that I'm coming to find in Him because all I have is Him. I never confuse whose voice that leads me because it's only His I've had to listen to. While I wish so many times my journey went so differently, I thank Him because in spite of He loves and uses me. Right before I sent this for publishing, the movie *Fighting Temptations* came on and they sang the song, "I Ain't Good Enough" at the end that speaks the very sentiments of my heart.

Chorus:

"Seems like I always fall short of being worthy

'Cause I ain't good enough

But He still loves me

I ain't no superstar

The spotlight ain't shining on me

(no, no, no, no)

Cause I ain't good enough

But He still loves me"

God, I've done plenty to be disqualified, but You still choose me. He still chooses you. Ministry has been hard and still is from time to time. I have enough prophesy of what God is going to do with me to fill my cup. Some I've still yet to see, but I still trust Him. I've asked myself at times was it me that kept the promise from manifesting? Did I delay it? Then my question switches to prayer. Lord, I pray I didn't destroy it. Every day is not promised to bring sunshine but even in the rain, still know you're purposed. Fires that come and the floods that grow, you are still purposed. Plenty will try to steal your joy, peace, and hope, but don't let them. I am a living witness that there is an after this. After the fire, after the flood, after the mountain and the valley, after all, still stand. Still hold fast to God's Word and never doubt. Winds will blow and storms will come, but God promised that you would make it to the other side. I'm here writing to you now, as a vessel God is perfecting every day. You, who is sitting here reading this, is a vessel God is perfecting every day. I say again, all will seem to rise against you, and some you will succumb to. God's Word still says the same, that you shall be on the other side. I never thought I would have a ministry that blesses thousands around the world. That I would be called to rise up a network of women, around the world, who are established to build each other up. That I

124

would meet amazing men and women of God and have them come and minister. People I believed I would never meet and at one time, I never even knew. I was sheltered from the dynamic voices of the world and now I have the opportunities to be blessed by them. Oh yeah, there is no stopping what God destined. There is nothing that can kill what God anointed to live. I am living proof. I am in my after this! 1 Peter 5:10-11 NKJV says, "But may the God of all grace, who called us to His eternal glory by Christ Jesus, after you have suffered a while, perfect, establish, strengthen, and settle you. To Him be the glory and the dominion forever and ever. Amen."

JOURNAL

Many days when I had no one to talk to besides God, I talked to my journal. You have lived such a victorious life, yet sometimes the things we deal with overshadow our ability to see it. I ended this book with some pages for you to journal your heart, as I have shared mine in these pages with you. I pray this has blessed you, that you have received your healing and that you come to see all God has for you.

_____

_____

_____

_____

_____

_____

_____

_____

_____

_____

_____

EPILOGUE

The Mask and The Mirror

...Revealing for a New Beginning

From childhood, one of my favorite Disney movies is "Snow White and The Seven Dwarfs." For many, the idea of the happily ever after brought great nostalgia to all who watched. Funny thing is I didn't get caught up in the happily ever after. My thoughts focused on the queen and the mirror. Of course not as a child watching, but I was certainly drawn as an adult. I mean, was I the only one who saw what was happening here? Here was this beautiful woman, being made queen, struggling with self-esteem so much, that she sought validation from a magic mirror. An item, no matter how magical, that truly had no idea what it's like to feel nor any understanding of what she contended with inside. Oh, how familiar this behavior was to me. Myself, along with so many others, seek validation of our worth, and our value from outside sources. No matter how magical the feeling was that we felt from their validation, truth is, they had no clue how we felt or possibly who we really were. They were telling us what we wanted to hear, instead of what we needed and that being the truth. We hinged our opinion of ourselves based on what they had to say. The question why is all I can ask myself today. Why did the "they's" matter so much? I could scream right here because I am so sick of "they." You know who "they" are. "They said this" and "they said that." Every time you turn around, "they" is showing up in everything. Yet, this same "they" is somehow nowhere to be found when it's time to be called to the carpet. How foolish it sounds today, but that was my life source once upon a time. I don't know about your "they," but my "they" weren't just anyone. I somehow found myself leaning on the validation of people who had no thoughts concerning themselves. They were blind to their own destiny, yet I was seeking them to proofread mine. Those who absolutely had no personal drive, but had hopes they would push me to my destiny. I'm most positive you are familiar with what I'm saying.

Here was a queen who couldn't have seen herself more than a servant. It can't be possible if she had to go through those measures just to feel good about who she was. There were unspoken words of her heart that I could hear loud and clear. I've always been my worst enemy. If there was criticism to be given, I gave it. If there was an impossible standard to set, I set it. While it is great to have self-truth, what I told myself was more destructive than helpful. For many of us, and I dare not limit it to men or women, we give ourselves the hardest time. We take our stumbles and make them life sentences. And heaven forbid we are surrounded by Negative Nancy's; they will be sure to constantly remind us of our shortcomings. They stay so enthralled with our "remember when," that they miss who we are or are becoming now.

When looking up the definition of a mirror, it is stated to be a reflective surface, that reflects a clear image. When looking in a mirror, what we see is supposed to be a clear depiction of reality or truth. For many years, I hated who I saw when I looked in the mirror. That person was ugly to me. I believed that so much, I could put my eyeliner on without ever looking at my face. The questions here are:

- Was the mirror reflecting real truth or my personal truth?
- When you look in the mirror, who is it that you see? Do you see the fearfully and wonderfully made person God designed you to be? Or do you see all your mistakes and every flaw?

The purpose of the mirror is to reflect truth. Can I be honest right here? I honestly believe the reason I saw ugly is because I didn't like who I was at that time. I believe the reason I couldn't look at my face was because I was ashamed of the person who was looking back at me. That was the truth. People have a problem with facing the truth. So we avoid it or we sugar coat it. We do whatever we can imagine to do just so we don't face it. In my book, I made reference to how I avoided accepting I was in jail.

I was convinced this was a mistake. Any moment I was going to be released. It took me eight months before I grasped the reality that I was sentenced to time in jail. I didn't want to face the truth. It took me having a break down before I was able to break out; break out of the fantasy I created for myself; to break out of the lies I was telling myself. And to break out of being the victim, so that I could finally become the victor.

One of the concepts I want to raise is something I've come to call "funhouse faith." If you are familiar with a funhouse mirror, it was an attraction at a carnival, that caused the image in it to be distorted. The tricks that it was able to do was to bring laughter and fun. Having this type of perception when it comes to life is really not so fun. Here is what I mean. Things that happen in life can cause you to seriously doubt the things God has spoken concerning it. You are promised to live a prosperous life, but allows to you fall into a financial bind. The very thoughts of prosperity go out the window because all you see is poverty. You are promised love; however, the person you are with cheats. Now your hopes of a happily ever after blow in the wind. Whatever challenges life throws, it seriously alters your faith. It takes the reality and distorts it. Now you are walking around believing based on an illusion, instead of on the certainty given to you by God. Now, your pain dictates your life. Your fear, worry and doubt all take lead in governing the direction you take. A funhouse mirror illusion is only temporary. Once you step back in front of a real mirror, the reflection returns to normal. Imagine if you allowed your entire self-image to be altered based off a temporary illusion.

Can I bring that to present day and circumstances? Someone doesn't agree with you. Now you believe you are completely wrong. Someone decides to not support you. Now you want to give up all together. Someone walks away from you. Now you decide to never let anyone else in your heart again. I can go on and on because I lived it. It brings pleasure to the enemy to see us suffer and live a life that is less than what God destines. He takes great pleasure in us dwelling in our weakness, instead of overcoming it through God's strength. I don't care what man says, God says, "fearfully and wonderfully made." I don't care what man doesn't agree with. God said, "You shall be the head and not the tail, above and not beneath; the lender and never again the borrower." God said that your works will bring you praise in the gates.

I have an exercise that I want you to do. Go and purchase a mirror from the Dollar Tree or wherever you decide. Purchase one that you can write or attach things to. That is why I didn't suggest using your bedroom or bathroom mirror, unless you are okay with things being all over them. You will also need a pack of post-it notes and a writing instrument. On the post it notes, I want you to write one word about the reflection that you see in the mirror. Be honest or this will not work otherwise. Your reflection is not limited to your physical qualities. Write about the emotions you see, the thoughts, whatever it is you see. Once you have done that, I want you to look at the words. For every negative word you placed, I want you to do two things:

- First, I want you to write a positive response. If you wrote ugly, write on there as well beautiful or pretty.
- Second, I want you to write a scripture or positive affirmation to accompany the change you made on that note.

Once complete, I want you to place those notes on your mirror. Every time you look in this mirror, you are changing your outlook on who you see. Your input of what the word you wrote or what your affirmation is instilling, is what is bringing about the change. You are using truth to conquer your lie. You are changing your distortion back to the truth. It's not something that will be easy. It wasn't for me and there are days I have to make myself look in the mirror. It's on those days I don't like myself so much.

Let me help you with a thought right here. If you think doing this once you are cured overnight, you are wrong. It's a daily decision that will bring about change. The bible tells us that we have to die to our flesh daily because with each new day, new challenges also come. These challenges don't come to play fair or treat you nice. They come to kill, steal and destroy. It is up to us to remember that God came that we might have life and one of more abundance. So when the devil comes to use our hearts or our minds against us, it's up to us to take authority over him. Put your mirror in a place where you will see it. Don't pack it away in a box or put it up on a shelf. Keep your mirror near. Overtime, you will look into it without giving it a thought. Each time the struggle will become less and less. If there's someone looking back at you who you do not like, then change them. If there is something about that person looking back at you that you don't like, then change it. In the midst of changing, make sure you are giving yourself a real chance. No one is perfect, but we have the privilege of being perfected in Him. The bible says God will give us beauty for our ashes, but He can't do it if we don't first turn them over to Him.

A mirror causes us to deal with lies we tell ourselves but what about a mask? I would be certain to say a mask allows us to tell lies to everyone else, while hiding the truth behind. My son loves Halloween because he enjoys being able to dress up. For that one day, he gets to be the superhero or creepy thing that he loves for the moment. For all of the religious ones, that statement wasn't for you. But before you send me to hell, remember you were once a kid too and things we come to learn as an adult, we weren't supposed to know or care about as a child. I teach my son, but I don't strip him in the process. During Christmas, he knows that mommy pays for things but I don't steal his joy that he feels about Santa. He's eight, so there you go. Anyway, back to my point.

For that one day, he gets to be someone else. Well, for many every day is Halloween. Before they leave out of their homes for the day, they put on the mask they want everyone to see. Whoever they decide to be is who we see. And, I was the Queen of that! There were so many days I cried and walked around hurt, I have lost count. I believe there wasn't one day of my marriage that I didn't cry and ask God to help me. But when I showed up at work, church and around our friends, there would be the biggest smile on my face. I would laugh with them and even play games with them. Then as soon as I got out of their sight, I could turn it off. With tears in my eyes, I am telling you that it was a miserable existence. I got so good at putting it on, I don't remember when I ever turned it off. I had no clue who I was. Today, I am still trying to figure out who I am. How many times can you remember putting on a mask? How many times can you say now you still put them on from time to time? There were so many days I was sitting around people hurting and they never knew. Your sister and your brother sitting around you are hurting and we miss it almost every time. Every smile is not happy nor is every tear sad.

Let's jump into another exercise. Get a mask and a marker. On the face of the mask, write all of the things we allow others to see. On the inside of the mask, write things that we hide from others. As you are writing, I want you to pray over your mask. I want you to ask God to help you with the barriers you have built in your life. The things that you hide are not necessarily meant for you to share. It does represent a wall that you've built that you now desire to take down. Your mask is your wall that is maybe keeping people out, but remember it is also holding you hostage within. So as you write, pray for God to remove the wall. For the things that you hide, apply scripture to for deliverance. Pray the scriptures. The bible declares that "this kind comes out by fasting and prayer" (Matthew

17:21). Our wounds and hurts are deep. Therefore, it's going to take depth to bring deliverance. After you have written and after you have prayed, then I want you to throw away your mask. Don't put it up to pull it back out. Throw it away. Often times the enemy can creep back in because we leave him a peep hole. Make the decision, once free always free. That there is no next time with this. This is your LAST TIME! Whom the son sets free is free indeed (Mark 10:45). There is liberty waiting on you. He already paid the price for us. All we have to do is receive our liberty and walk in it.

This is only a portion of all that I would desire to share. It's something I'm evolving into a complete manuscript for seminars to share. The greatest message I have ever ministered was through the miracle worked out of the mess of my life. I know about the mirror and I most definitely know about the mask. I also understand liberty and walking in freedom. There is nothing like it. If my wounds can bring someone healing, then my living is not in vain. I pray this snippet blessed you. I pray the entire book blessed you. There is a special grace one must walk in when your transparency proves to bless others. It's a gift I dare not take for granted and one I shall cherish and share all the days of my life. God's richest blessings to you!

~Overseer Kimberly McWilliams~

KVM Global "Ministering H.O.P.E. to the World"

MEET THE AUTHOR

Overseer Kimberly McWilliams is a native of Queens, New York. She is the mother of two beautiful children, Adrienne Makayla and Lannice Oreonne. Kimberly began ministry singing at the age of three. She did, what came to be known, her first sermon at the age of eight. Through the years she has been licensed as a Minister, Evangelist and Elder. In 2010, she was installed as Pastor and both of her ministries, Remnants of the Kingdom International Ministries and KVM Global Ministries, were established. In 2015 she was elevated to Overseer, and Healing House Assembly of Ministries was established.

In 2018, Kimberly published her first book, *Eliminating Blessing Blockers*. The focus of the book is to address and conquer barriers that keep us from living a prosperous life. While this may be her first book published, it is actually the second book the Lord had her release. The first being *Mid-Day Munchies*, 10 short stories that empower the reader's day and life.

Kimberly is the Founder and Visionary of A Woman Who Knows Her Worth Women's Network. She is also the establishmentarian of a bi-coastal ministry, KVM Global East (Maryland) and KVM Global West (California).

Contact Information:

Website: www.kvmglobal.com

Email Address: kvmministries2015@gmail.com

Address: PO Box 28585 Henrico, VA 23228

Facebook: Kimberly McWilliams

Facebook Page: KVM Global Ministries

Facebook Group: A Woman Who Knows Her Worth

Instagram: kvmcwilliams